THURSDAY

IS

POT LUCK

from Hearty Casseroles to Stir-Fries to Main-Course Salads

◆　◆　◆

TIME-LIFE BOOKS, ALEXANDRIA, VIRGINIA

TIME-LIFE BOOKS IS A DIVISION OF TIME LIFE INC.

PRESIDENT and CEO, Time Life Inc.	John M. Fahey Jr.
PRESIDENT, Time-Life Books	John D. Hall

TIME-LIFE CUSTOM PUBLISHING

VICE PRESIDENT and PUBLISHER	Terry Newell
Director of Sales	Neil Levin
Director of New Product Development	Regina Hall
Managing Editor	Donia Ann Steele
Editorial Director	Jennifer Pearce
Senior Art Director	Christopher M. Register
Sales Manager	Liz Ziehl
Retail Promotions Manager	Gary Stoiber
Associate Marketing Manager	Dana A. Coleman
Operations Manager	Valerie Lewis
Director of Financial Operations	J. Brian Birky
Financial Analyst	Trish Palini
Production Manager	Carolyn Bounds
Quality Assurance Manager	Miriam P. Newton
Executive Assistant	Tammy York

Produced by Rebus, Inc.
New York, New York

Illustrations
William Neeper

Library of Congress Cataloging-in-Publication Data
Thursday is pot luck: from hearty casseroles to stir-fries to main-course salads.
p. cm. -- (The Everyday cookbooks)
Includes index.
ISBN 0-8094-9189-3
ISBN 0-7835-4780-3
1. Entrées (Cookery) 2. Quick and easy cookery. I. Time-Life Books.
II. Series.
TX740.T45   1995
641.5'55--dc20
95-18646
CIP

Introduction

Remember when you could tell what day of the week it was by what Mom was making for dinner? It was predictable, and comforting, and—as far as Mom was concerned—efficient. But every now and then, didn't you wish she would give her usual casserole recipe a rest and try something new? Now here's a cookbook that not only helps you plan meals like Mom used to make but gives you a wonderful variety of recipes, too. With *Thursday Is Pot Luck* you can offer your family a delightfully different one-dish meal every week.

To make life even easier, this cookbook includes the following features:

- There are no difficult techniques or exotic ingredients. All of the recipes can be made with supermarket-available foods, and a great many of them can be made entirely with ingredients already in the pantry.

- Each recipe is designed with everyone's busy schedule in mind, with many taking under 45 minutes to prepare. These recipes are labeled "Extra-Quick" and are marked with this symbol: ◆ (A full listing of the extra-quick recipes is included in the index under the heading Extra-Quick.)

- Many of the recipes include lower-fat alternatives, such as reduced-fat sour cream and low-fat milk. In addition, we have created a number of recipes that get fewer than 30 percent of their calories from fat. These recipes are labeled "Low-Fat" and are marked with this symbol: ◇ (A full listing of the low-fat recipes is included in the index under the heading Low-Fat.)

- As a further help to the cook, there are notes throughout the book that provide simple variations on recipes, cooking shortcuts or tips on how to lower fat, suggestions for simple desserts that can be made for weekday meals, and substitutions, in case you can't find (or don't like) certain ingredients.

- In a special section called "Family Favorites," we include recipes that even the pickiest eaters will like, such as Chicken Drumsticks Cacciatore and Tex-Mex Macaroni and Cheese.

But best of all, in *Thursday Is Pot Luck* there are enough delicious one-dish recipes for more than two years' worth of Thursdays!

Contents

Pies and Pizzas

Main-Course Salads

Family Favorites

Index

Spinach Soup with Ravioli and Parmesan Toasts

SERVES 4

◆ EXTRA-QUICK

1 TABLESPOON PLUS 2 TEASPOONS
   OLIVE OIL
1 MEDIUM RED ONION, CUT INTO THIN
   WEDGES
2 GARLIC CLOVES, MINCED
2 MEDIUM CARROTS, CUT INTO
   2-INCH-LONG MATCHSTICKS
4 CUPS REDUCED-SODIUM CHICKEN
   BROTH

1 TEASPOON BASIL
¼ TEASPOON BLACK PEPPER
PINCH OF RED PEPPER FLAKES
2 SLICES FIRM-TEXTURED WHITE BREAD
2 TABLESPOONS GRATED PARMESAN
   CHEESE
1 POUND CHEESE-FILLED RAVIOLI
¼ POUND FRESH SPINACH, TORN INTO
   LARGE PIECES

1. In a large saucepan, warm 1 tablespoon of the oil over medium-high heat. Add the onion and garlic, and stir-fry until the onion begins to brown, about 5 minutes.

2. Add the carrots, broth, basil, black pepper, and red pepper flakes, and bring the mixture to a boil.

3. Meanwhile, preheat the broiler or a toaster oven. Sprinkle the bread with the Parmesan and drizzle on the remaining 2 teaspoons oil. Toast under the broiler or in the toaster oven for 2 minutes, or until golden. Cut each slice into 8 triangles.

4. When the broth has come to a boil, add the ravioli and cook until the ravioli is al dente according to package directions. One minute before the ravioli is done, add the spinach. Stir to wilt the spinach, and remove from the heat.

5. Serve the soup topped with the Parmesan toasts.

PROVENÇALE VEGETABLE SOUP

SERVES 6

9 GARLIC CLOVES, PEELED

⅓ CUP PLUS 2 TABLESPOONS OLIVE OIL

1 MEDIUM ONION, COARSELY CHOPPED

1 LARGE CARROT, COARSELY CHOPPED

1 CELERY RIB, COARSELY CHOPPED

4 CUPS REDUCED-SODIUM CHICKEN
  BROTH

2 SMALL UNPEELED RED POTATOES,
  COARSELY CHOPPED

¼ POUND GREEN BEANS, COARSELY
  CHOPPED

¼ POUND CABBAGE, COARSELY
  CHOPPED

1 SMALL ZUCCHINI, COARSELY
  CHOPPED

2 TEASPOONS THYME

1 TEASPOON FENNEL SEEDS

1 BAY LEAF

½ TEASPOON BLACK PEPPER

¾ CUP (PACKED) FRESH BASIL LEAVES

2 MEDIUM TOMATOES, COARSELY
  CHOPPED

ONE 19-OUNCE CAN WHITE KIDNEY
  BEANS, RINSED AND DRAINED

ONE 10-OUNCE PACKAGE FROZEN BABY
  LIMA BEANS

1 CUP FROZEN PEAS

½ CUP GRATED PARMESAN CHEESE

1. Mince 3 of the garlic cloves and set aside. Place the remaining 6 garlic cloves in a food processor; set aside.

2. In a large saucepan, warm 1 tablespoon of the oil over medium-high heat. Add the onion and minced garlic, and stir-fry for 3 minutes. Add 1 tablespoon of the oil and the carrot and celery, and stir-fry until the onion is golden, about 5 minutes.

3. Add the broth, potatoes, green beans, cabbage, zucchini, thyme, fennel seeds, bay leaf, and pepper, and bring to a boil. Reduce the heat to low, cover, and simmer for 5 minutes.

4. Meanwhile, add the basil to the garlic in the food processor and mince together. With the processor running, pour in the remaining ⅓ cup oil. Set the basil-garlic sauce aside.

5. Return the soup to a boil over medium-high heat. Add the tomatoes, white kidney beans, lima beans, and peas, and let return to a boil. Cook until the limas and peas are heated through, about 3 minutes.

6. Just before serving, remove and discard the bay leaf. Stir the basil-garlic sauce into the soup. Serve with the Parmesan on the side.

Spicy Lentil-Vegetable Soup

SERVES 4

◇ LOW-FAT

2 TEASPOONS VEGETABLE OIL

1 LARGE ONION, COARSELY CHOPPED

5 GARLIC CLOVES, MINCED

2 TABLESPOONS CURRY POWDER

1 TEASPOON GROUND CORIANDER

1 TEASPOON CUMIN

1 CUP LENTILS, RINSED AND PICKED OVER

4 CUPS REDUCED-SODIUM CHICKEN BROTH

ONE 16-OUNCE CAN NO-SALT-ADDED WHOLE TOMATOES

ONE 10-OUNCE PACKAGE FROZEN CHOPPED SPINACH

1 MEDIUM ZUCCHINI, COARSELY CHOPPED

¼ CUP REDUCED-FAT SOUR CREAM

1. In a medium saucepan, warm the oil over medium-high heat. Add the onion and garlic, and stir-fry until the onion begins to brown, about 5 minutes.

2. Add the curry powder, coriander, and cumin, and cook, stirring, until the spices are fragrant, about 1 minute.

3. Add the lentils, broth, tomatoes, and spinach, and bring to a boil over medium-high heat, breaking up the tomatoes with the back of a spoon. Reduce the heat to low, cover, and simmer until the lentils are tender, 25 to 30 minutes, stirring occasionally to break up the spinach.

4. Add the zucchini to the soup and cook until heated through, about 5 minutes.

5. Serve the soup with the sour cream on the side.

Variation: *To complement the Indian seasonings in the soup, replace the sour cream topping with the easy-to-make Indian condiment called raita. Cucumber raita, one of the most popular types, is made by stirring shredded (and well-drained) cucumber into plain yogurt. Add some chopped fresh cilantro or fresh mint, a pinch of cumin and salt, and a tiny pinch of cayenne.*

South-of-the-Border Black Bean Soup

SERVES 4

◆ EXTRA-QUICK   ◇ LOW-FAT

1 TABLESPOON VEGETABLE OIL

1 MEDIUM ONION, COARSELY CHOPPED

2 GARLIC CLOVES, MINCED

TWO 16-OUNCE CANS BLACK BEANS, RINSED AND DRAINED

ONE 10-OUNCE PACKAGE FROZEN CORN KERNELS, THAWED

2¾ CUPS CHICKEN BROTH, PREFERABLY REDUCED-SODIUM

1 TABLESPOON CHILI POWDER

1½ TEASPOONS OREGANO

PINCH OF CAYENNE PEPPER

1 BAY LEAF

¼ CUP CHOPPED CILANTRO (OPTIONAL)

½ CUP REDUCED-FAT SOUR CREAM (OPTIONAL)

1. In a large saucepan, warm the oil over medium-high heat. Add the onion and garlic, and sauté until the onion begins to brown, about 5 minutes.

2. Stir in the beans, corn, broth, chili powder, oregano, cayenne, and bay leaf. Cover and bring the mixture to a boil. Reduce the heat to medium-low, cover, and simmer for 15 minutes. Remove and discard the bay leaf.

3. Just before serving, use a slotted spoon to transfer about 1½ cups of the solids to a blender or food processor, and purée until smooth. Return the purée to the soup and simmer over low heat until warmed through.

4. Serve the soup with a sprinkling of cilantro and a dollop of sour cream, if desired.

VEGETABLE SOUP
WITH GRILLED CHICKEN

SERVES 4

½ POUND CHICKEN CUTLETS

1 TABLESPOON PLUS 1 TEASPOON OLIVE
OIL

2 TABLESPOONS FRESH LIME JUICE

¼ TEASPOON BLACK PEPPER

1 LARGE RED ONION, CHOPPED

2 GARLIC CLOVES, FINELY CHOPPED

6 CUPS REDUCED-SODIUM CHICKEN
BROTH

ONE 16-OUNCE CAN NO-SALT-ADDED
WHOLE TOMATOES, DRAINED

½ TEASPOON OREGANO

¼ TEASPOON CUMIN

¼ TEASPOON SALT

⅛ TEASPOON GROUND CORIANDER

⅛ TEASPOON CAYENNE PEPPER

3 CORN TORTILLAS

1 MEDIUM CARROT, JULIENNED

1 SMALL ZUCCHINI, JULIENNED

1 SMALL YELLOW SQUASH, JULIENNED

1 TABLESPOON MINCED CHIVES

1. Set the chicken on a plate, drizzle with 1 teaspoon of the oil and the lime juice, and sprinkle with the pepper. Let the chicken marinate while you make the rest of the soup.

2. In a saucepan, combine the onion, garlic, and broth, and bring to a boil over medium-high heat. Add the tomatoes, oregano, cumin, salt, coriander, and cayenne, and break up the tomatoes with the back of a spoon. Reduce the heat to low and simmer for 20 minutes.

3. Meanwhile, preheat the broiler. Brush the tortillas with the remaining 1 tablespoon oil and cut them into thin strips. Spread the strips on a baking sheet and broil 4 inches from the heat for 3 minutes, or until they are crisp and lightly browned. Set aside.

4. Remove the chicken from the marinade, place on the broiler rack, and broil for 2 minutes per side, or until firm to the touch. Cut the pieces on the diagonal into thin slices.

5. Add the carrot, zucchini, and yellow squash to the soup, and simmer them until they are tender, about 6 minutes.

6. Arrange the chicken slices on top of the soup and sprinkle it with the chives. Serve the tortilla strips in a bowl alongside.

Chicken, Eggplant, and Tomato Soup

SERVES 4

◇ LOW-FAT

2 OUNCES FETA CHEESE

8 CUPS REDUCED-SODIUM CHICKEN BROTH

4 GARLIC CLOVES, FINELY CHOPPED

2 TABLESPOONS FRESH LEMON JUICE

¼ TEASPOON BLACK PEPPER

1 POUND SKINLESS, BONELESS CHICKEN BREASTS

1 TABLESPOON CHOPPED FRESH MINT

ONE 28-OUNCE CAN NO-SALT-ADDED WHOLE TOMATOES, DRAINED

1 TABLESPOON FRESH THYME, OR ¾ TEASPOON DRIED

¾ POUND UNPEELED EGGPLANT, CUT INTO ½-INCH CUBES

1. In a shallow bowl, combine the feta and cold water to cover, then set aside for about 10 minutes to remove some of the salt. Drain the feta, crumble, and set aside.

2. Meanwhile, in a large saucepan, bring the broth to a boil over high heat. Add the garlic, 1 tablespoon of the lemon juice, and the pepper, and reduce the heat to low. Add the chicken and simmer gently until the meat feels springy to the touch, about 7 minutes.

3. Reserving the broth, transfer the chicken to a cutting board. Cut the chicken into small cubes and place the cubes in a medium bowl. Add the mint and remaining 1 tablespoon

lemon juice, toss to coat, and set the chicken aside to marinate while you cook the tomatoes and eggplant.

4. Add the tomatoes and thyme to the broth. Bring the mixture to a boil over high heat, breaking up the tomatoes with the back of a spoon. Reduce the heat to low and simmer, stirring occasionally, for 10 minutes.

5. Add the eggplant and cook until tender, about 5 minutes. Stir in the chicken and its marinade and simmer the soup until the chicken is heated through, about 2 minutes.

6. Serve the soup with the feta cheese sprinkled on top.

Turkey-Lentil Soup

SERVES 6

◇ LOW-FAT

1½ POUNDS TURKEY DRUMSTICKS,
    SKINNED
¼ TEASPOON BLACK PEPPER
2 TEASPOONS OLIVE OIL
1 SMALL ONION, THINLY SLICED
1 CUP LENTILS, RINSED AND PICKED
    OVER
1 SMALL BAY LEAF

1 SMALL CARROT, THINLY SLICED
1 SMALL ZUCCHINI, THINLY SLICED
1 SMALL CELERY RIB, THINLY SLICED
1 SMALL TOMATO, COARSELY CHOPPED
1 TEASPOON MINCED FRESH SAGE, OR
    ¼ TEASPOON DRIED
½ TEASPOON SALT

1. Sprinkle the drumsticks with the pepper. In a Dutch oven or flameproof casserole, warm the oil over medium heat. Add the drumsticks and cook, turning frequently, until they are evenly browned, 2 to 3 minutes. Push the drumsticks to one side of the pan, then add the onion and cook it until it is translucent, 2 to 3 minutes.

2. Add the lentils, 5 cups of water, and the bay leaf, and bring the mixture to a boil, skimming off any surface foam. Reduce the heat to low, cover, and cook, stirring occasionally, until the turkey is cooked through, about 40 minutes.

3. Transfer the drumsticks to a cutting board. When they are cool enough to handle, slice the meat from the bones and cut it into small pieces; discard the bones. Remove and discard the bay leaf.

4. Add the carrot, zucchini, celery, and tomato to the soup, and simmer for 5 minutes. Add the turkey meat, sage, and salt, and cook the soup until the vegetables are tender, about 2 minutes. Serve hot.

Turkey-Mushroom Chowder

SERVES 4

3½ CUPS REDUCED-SODIUM CHICKEN
  BROTH
1 POUND SKINLESS, BONELESS TURKEY
  BREAST
1½ TEASPOONS OREGANO
¼ TEASPOON BLACK PEPPER
1 TABLESPOON OLIVE OIL
3 GARLIC CLOVES, MINCED
1 MEDIUM ONION, COARSELY CHOPPED

2 TABLESPOONS UNSALTED BUTTER
½ CUP RICE
1 MEDIUM CARROT, COARSELY
  CHOPPED
¾ POUND MUSHROOMS, COARSELY
  CHOPPED
3 TABLESPOONS FLOUR
1 CUP LOW-FAT MILK

1. In a medium saucepan, bring the broth to a boil over high heat.

2. Meanwhile, cut the turkey into 8 equal pieces to shorten the cooking time.

3. Add the turkey pieces, oregano, and pepper to the boiling broth. Let the broth return to a boil, then reduce the heat to medium-low, cover, and simmer until the turkey is cooked through, about 15 minutes. Transfer the turkey to a plate and cover loosely with foil to keep warm. Set the broth aside.

4. Meanwhile, in another medium saucepan, warm the oil over medium-high heat. Add the garlic and onion, and cook, stirring often, until the onion has softened slightly, about 3 minutes.

5. Add the butter, rice, carrot, and mushrooms, and cook, stirring, for 3 minutes. Stir in the flour and cook, stirring, until the flour is no longer visible, about 30 seconds. Add the reserved broth and bring the mixture to a boil. Reduce the heat to medium-low, cover, and simmer until the rice is tender, about 20 minutes.

6. Meanwhile, cut the turkey into bite-size pieces. When the rice is cooked, return the chowder to a boil over medium-high heat. Add the turkey and milk, and cook, stirring, until heated through, about 2 minutes.

BEEF GOULASH SOUP

SERVES 4

2 TABLESPOONS OLIVE OIL

1 MEDIUM ONION, COARSELY CHOPPED

2 GARLIC CLOVES, MINCED

½ POUND LEAN GROUND BEEF

3 CUPS TOMATO JUICE

1¾ CUPS BEEF BROTH

2 TEASPOONS PAPRIKA

½ TEASPOON BLACK PEPPER

¾ POUND UNPEELED RED POTATOES, DICED

1 SMALL GREEN BELL PEPPER, DICED

1 SMALL RED BELL PEPPER, DICED

1. In a large saucepan, warm the oil over medium-high heat. Add the onion and garlic, and sauté until the onion is just translucent, about 2 minutes.

2. Crumble the ground beef into the pan and cook, breaking up the meat with a spoon, until the meat just begins to brown, 5 to 10 minutes.

3. Add the tomato juice, broth, paprika, black pepper, and potatoes, and stir well. Bring the mixture to a boil, reduce the heat to medium-low, cover, and simmer, stirring occasionally, for 10 minutes.

4. Stir in the bell peppers and cook until the flavors are blended and the potatoes are tender, about 10 minutes. Serve hot.

BEEF AND BARLEY SOUP

SERVES 6

◇ LOW-FAT

ONE 16-OUNCE CAN NO-SALT-ADDED
   WHOLE TOMATOES
3 CUPS BEEF BROTH
¼ CUP PEARL BARLEY
2 GARLIC CLOVES, MINCED
1 TEASPOON SUGAR
¾ TEASPOON THYME

¼ TEASPOON BLACK PEPPER
1 BAY LEAF
¾ POUND LEAN STEWING BEEF, CUT
   INTO ¾-INCH CUBES
3 MEDIUM CARROTS, DICED
½ POUND SMALL MUSHROOMS
1 CUP FROZEN PEARL ONIONS

1. In a large saucepan, combine the tomatoes, broth, ½ cup of water, barley, garlic, sugar, thyme, pepper, and bay leaf. Bring the liquid to a boil over medium-high heat, breaking up the tomatoes with the back of a spoon.

2. Add the beef, carrots, mushrooms, and pearl onions. Return the soup to a boil, reduce the heat to medium-low, cover, and simmer, stirring occasionally, until the barley is tender, about 55 minutes.

3. Remove and discard the bay leaf before serving.

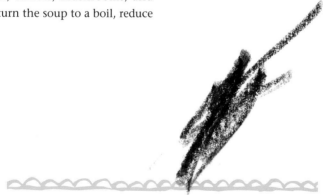

SUBSTITUTION: *If you can get fresh pearl onions, by all means use them instead of frozen. To peel the fresh ones easily, blanch the onions in boiling water for a minute or two, and they'll slip right out of their skins. But if you can't find pearl onions of any type, substitute quartered yellow, red, or white onions; the flavor will be the same.*

Beefy Tortellini Soup

SERVES 4

♦ EXTRA-QUICK

1 TABLESPOON OLIVE OIL

1 MEDIUM ONION, COARSELY CHOPPED

2 GARLIC CLOVES, MINCED

¼ POUND LEAN GROUND BEEF

2½ CUPS BEEF BROTH

1 CUP CANNED CRUSHED TOMATOES

2 MEDIUM CARROTS, THINLY SLICED

1 TEASPOON BASIL

¼ TEASPOON BLACK PEPPER

½ POUND CHEESE-FILLED TORTELLINI

1 MEDIUM ZUCCHINI, HALVED
   LENGTHWISE AND CUT CROSSWISE
   INTO THIN HALF-ROUNDS

¼ CUP GRATED PARMESAN CHEESE

1. In a medium saucepan, warm the oil over medium-high heat. Add the onion and garlic, and stir-fry until the mixture just begins to brown, about 3 minutes. Crumble in the beef and cook, stirring, until the meat is no longer pink, about 3 minutes.

2. Add the broth, 1½ cups of water, and the tomatoes. Bring the mixture to a boil over medium-high heat. Add the carrots, basil, and pepper, and cook, stirring occasionally, for 2 minutes.

3. Add the tortellini and cook until al dente according to package directions.

4. Three minutes before the tortellini are done, add the zucchini to the soup. Cook, stirring occasionally, until the zucchini is crisp-tender.

5. Serve the soup with the Parmesan cheese on the side.

Kitchen Note: *The cooking time for the tortellini depends upon whether they're fresh or dried. Fresh cheese tortellini, which you'll find in the dairy case at most supermarkets, take 7 to 12 minutes to cook. Dry tortellini, which you'll find on the shelf with other dried pastas, can take 3 to 5 minutes longer.*

New Mexican Pork Soup with Fresh Salsa

SERVES 4

1 TABLESPOON OLIVE OIL

1 POUND LEAN BONELESS PORK, CUT
INTO ¾-INCH CUBES

1½ CUPS BOILING WATER

½ TEASPOON SALT

1 POUND CHICKEN THIGHS, SKINNED

2 MEDIUM ONIONS, COARSELY
CHOPPED

4 GARLIC CLOVES, PEELED AND HALVED

¼ TEASPOON WHOLE BLACK
PEPPERCORNS

ONE 16-OUNCE CAN WHITE HOMINY,
RINSED AND DRAINED

¾ POUND TOMATOES, COARSELY
CHOPPED

3 PICKLED JALAPEÑOS, SEEDED AND
MINCED

3 TABLESPOONS CHOPPED CILANTRO

1 TEASPOON FRESH LIME JUICE

1 TEASPOON OREGANO

2 LIMES, CUT INTO WEDGES

1 SMALL HEAD OF CABBAGE, SHREDDED

1 CUP CHOPPED SCALLIONS

6 TO 8 RADISHES, SLIVERED

1. In a large saucepan, warm the oil over medium-high heat. Add the pork cubes and cook, stirring frequently, until evenly browned, 5 to 7 minutes.

2. Pour in the boiling water; stir in the salt. Add the chicken, all but ½ cup of the onions, the garlic, and peppercorns. Stir, reduce the heat to medium-low, cover, and simmer until the chicken is tender, about 30 minutes. Transfer the chicken to a bowl and set aside.

3. Stir the hominy into the soup, cover, and simmer, stirring occasionally, for 20 minutes.

4. Meanwhile, in a medium bowl, combine the tomatoes, jalapeños, cilantro, lime juice, oregano, and reserved ½ cup onion. Set the salsa aside.

5. Return the chicken to the soup and cook until the chicken is heated through, about 3 minutes.

6. Serve the soup with separate bowls of lime wedges, cabbage, scallions, radishes, and salsa for garnishes.

CHINESE HOT POT

SERVES 4

◆ EXTRA-QUICK

2 TEASPOONS ORIENTAL (DARK)
  SESAME OIL
5 QUARTER-SIZE SLICES FRESH GINGER,
  MINCED
3 GARLIC CLOVES, MINCED
¼ POUND LEAN GROUND PORK
ONE 19-OUNCE CAN CHICK-PEAS,
  RINSED AND DRAINED
2½ CUPS CHICKEN BROTH, PREFERABLY
  REDUCED-SODIUM
ONE 8-OUNCE CAN SLICED BAMBOO
  SHOOTS, DRAINED

ONE 8-OUNCE CAN SLICED WATER
  CHESTNUTS, DRAINED
1 TABLESPOON REDUCED-SODIUM SOY
  SAUCE
2 DROPS OF HOT PEPPER SAUCE
½ TEASPOON RED PEPPER FLAKES
2 TABLESPOONS CORNSTARCH
¼ POUND FRESH OR FROZEN SNOW
  PEAS
¼ POUND FIRM TOFU, CUBED
  (OPTIONAL)
¼ CUP MINCED CILANTRO

1. In a large saucepan, warm the sesame oil over medium-high heat. Add the ginger and garlic, and stir-fry until fragrant, about 1 minute. Crumble in the ground pork and stir-fry until the meat begins to brown, about 3 minutes.

2. Add the chick-peas, 2 cups of the broth, the bamboo shoots, water chestnuts, soy sauce, hot pepper sauce, and red pepper flakes. Bring the mixture to a boil over medium heat.

3. Meanwhile, in a small bowl, blend the cornstarch with the remaining ½ cup broth.

4. When the soup has come to a boil, stir in the cornstarch mixture, the snow peas, and tofu (if using). Cook, stirring, until the soup has thickened slightly and the snow peas are cooked through, 2 to 3 minutes.

5. Stir in the cilantro and serve hot.

Potato-Cabbage Soup with Ham

SERVES 4

◆ EXTRA-QUICK

4 TABLESPOONS UNSALTED BUTTER

1 POUND ALL-PURPOSE POTATOES,
PEELED AND DICED

2 MEDIUM CARROTS, DICED

8 SCALLIONS, COARSELY CHOPPED

3 TABLESPOONS FLOUR

4 CUPS SHREDDED CABBAGE

3½ CUPS REDUCED-SODIUM CHICKEN
BROTH

1 TEASPOON DILL

½ TEASPOON BLACK PEPPER

¼ POUND LEAN HAM, DICED

1. In a medium saucepan, warm the butter over medium heat until melted. Add the potatoes, carrots, and scallions, and sauté until the scallions are wilted, about 5 minutes. Stir in the flour and cook, stirring, until the flour is no longer visible, about 30 seconds.

2. Add the cabbage, broth, dill, and pepper, and bring the mixture to a boil over medium-high heat. Reduce the heat to medium-low, cover, and simmer, stirring occasionally, until

the cabbage, carrots, and potatoes are tender and the flavors blended, about 20 minutes.

3. Just before serving, lightly mash some of the vegetables in the saucepan with a potato masher to thicken the liquid, if desired. Stir in the ham and simmer until heated through, about 3 minutes.

Variation: *Replacing the white potatoes with sweet potatoes makes an interesting flavor change in this soup. The recipe is quite flexible overall: You could also leave out the cabbage (if it's not a family favorite) and substitute another potato, two more carrots, more scallions (to taste), and two diced celery ribs. Add the celery in Step 2 along with the broth.*

HAM, WHITE BEAN, AND SWEET POTATO SOUP

SERVES 4

◆ EXTRA-QUICK ◇ LOW-FAT

3½ CUPS REDUCED-SODIUM CHICKEN
    BROTH
2 GARLIC CLOVES, MINCED
1 TEASPOON DIJON MUSTARD
¼ TEASPOON BLACK PEPPER
1 BAY LEAF
1 MEDIUM SWEET POTATO, PEELED AND
    CUT INTO ½-INCH DICE

ONE 15-OUNCE CAN SMALL WHITE
    BEANS, RINSED AND DRAINED
½ POUND SMOKED HAM, SUCH AS
    BLACK FOREST, DICED
2 SCALLIONS, COARSELY CHOPPED

1. In a medium saucepan, bring the broth, garlic, mustard, pepper, and bay leaf to a boil over medium-high heat.

2. Add the sweet potato, and return the broth mixture to a boil. Reduce the heat to medium-low, cover, and simmer, stirring occasionally, until the sweet potato is tender, about 20 minutes.

3. Add the beans, ham, and scallions to the soup, and cook until heated through, about 2 minutes. Remove and discard the bay leaf before serving.

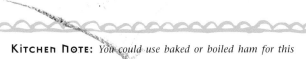

KITCHEN NOTE: *You could use baked or boiled ham for this soup, but Black Forest ham, which is smoked, makes the soup taste as if it has simmered for hours with a ham bone. If your deli does not offer Black Forest ham, see if another smoked ham is available.*

HAM AND LENTIL SOUP

SERVES 4

◇ LOW-FAT

2 TABLESPOONS OLIVE OIL

1 MEDIUM RED ONION, COARSELY
CHOPPED

2 GARLIC CLOVES, MINCED

2 MEDIUM CARROTS, COARSELY
CHOPPED

2 MEDIUM CELERY RIBS, COARSELY
CHOPPED

1½ CUPS LENTILS, RINSED AND PICKED
OVER

5 CUPS REDUCED-SODIUM CHICKEN
BROTH

1 TEASPOON OREGANO

¼ TEASPOON BLACK PEPPER

¼ POUND BOILED, BAKED, OR SMOKED
HAM, CUT INTO ½-INCH CUBES

1. In a medium saucepan, warm the oil over medium heat. Add the onion and garlic, and sauté, stirring occasionally, until the onion is softened and light brown, about 10 minutes.

2. Add the carrots, celery, lentils, broth, oregano, and pepper. Bring to a boil over medium-high heat. Reduce the heat to low, cover, and simmer, stirring occasionally, until the lentils are tender, about 30 minutes.

3. With a slotted spoon, transfer about 1 cup of the solids to a food processor or blender, and purée until smooth. Then stir the purée into the soup in the saucepan.

4. Add the ham to the soup and return it to a boil over medium-high heat. Serve hot.

Noodle Soup
with Carrots and Ham

SERVES 4

◆ EXTRA-QUICK ◇ LOW-FAT

7 CUPS REDUCED-SODIUM CHICKEN
   BROTH
4 QUARTER-SIZE SLICES FRESH GINGER
½ TEASPOON ORIENTAL (DARK) SESAME
   OIL
½ POUND ANGEL HAIR PASTA
¼ POUND UNSLICED LEAN HAM, CUT
   INTO 2-INCH-LONG MATCHSTICKS

4 ROMAINE LETTUCE LEAVES,
   SHREDDED
4 MEDIUM CARROTS, CUT INTO
   2-INCH-LONG MATCHSTICKS
2 MEDIUM ZUCCHINI, CUT INTO
   2-INCH-LONG MATCHSTICKS

1. In a large flameproof casserole, combine the broth, ginger, and sesame oil, and bring to a boil over medium-high heat.

2. Add the pasta to the boiling broth and cook until almost al dente, about 5 minutes.

3. Arrange the ham, lettuce, carrots, and zucchini on top of the soup, covering one-fourth of the surface with each ingredient. Cover the pot and cook until the lettuce is wilted and the ham is heated through, 2 to 3 minutes.

4. Bring the covered casserole to the table and serve the soup directly from the pan to display the pattern of ingredients on top. Or, ladle the broth into individual soup bowls along with some of each of the ingredients.

Quick Three-Bean Chili

SERVES 4

◆ EXTRA-QUICK

1 CUP CANNED KIDNEY BEANS, RINSED
AND DRAINED

1 CUP CANNED PINTO BEANS, RINSED
AND DRAINED

1 CUP CANNED BLACK BEANS, RINSED
AND DRAINED

ONE 14½-OUNCE CAN NO-SALT-ADDED
STEWED TOMATOES

2 CUPS CHICKEN BROTH, PREFERABLY
REDUCED-SODIUM

2 TABLESPOONS HOT SALSA

½ TEASPOON CUMIN

½ TEASPOON SALT

1 CUP SHREDDED CHEDDAR OR
MONTEREY JACK CHEESE

2 SCALLIONS, THINLY SLICED

2 TABLESPOONS CHOPPED CILANTRO

¼ CUP PITTED BLACK OLIVES, SLICED
INTO RINGS

⅓ CUP REDUCED-FAT SOUR CREAM

1. In a large saucepan, combine the beans, tomatoes, broth, salsa, and cumin. Stir to blend and bring to a boil over medium-high heat. Reduce the heat to medium-low and simmer, stirring occasionally, for 5 minutes. Stir in the salt.

2. To serve, ladle the chili into 4 bowls and garnish with the cheese, scallions, cilantro, olives, and sour cream.

KITCHEN NOTES: *The reasons for rinsing and draining canned beans are twofold: In addition to clarifying their flavors, the rinsing eliminates a considerable amount of the sodium that's added to their packing liquid. For the best selection of canned beans, check the Latin and Italian foods sections of your supermarket.*

CURRIED VEGETABLE STEW

SERVES 4

2 TABLESPOONS CORNSTARCH

4 CUPS REDUCED-SODIUM CHICKEN
BROTH

1½ TO 2 TABLESPOONS CURRY POWDER

2 TABLESPOONS UNSALTED BUTTER

½ POUND CARROTS, CUT ON THE
DIAGONAL INTO 1½-INCH-LONG
PIECES

1 POUND UNPEELED RED POTATOES,
CUT INTO 1½-INCH CHUNKS

1 LARGE ONION, CUT INTO 1½-INCH
CHUNKS

16 SMALL MUSHROOMS

1 CUP CANNED WHITE KIDNEY BEANS
(CANNELLINI), RINSED AND
DRAINED

1 CUP FROZEN PEAS

¼ CUP CASHEWS, COARSELY CHOPPED

2 TABLESPOONS REDUCED-SODIUM SOY
SAUCE

¼ TEASPOON SALT

1. In a small bowl, combine the cornstarch and 3 tablespoons of the broth, stir to blend, and set aside. In a cup, combine the curry powder and 1 tablespoon broth, and stir until a paste forms. Set aside.

2. In a large pot, warm the butter over medium-high heat until melted. Add the carrots, potatoes, and onion, and cook, stirring occasionally, for 4 minutes.

3. Stir in the remaining 3¾ cups broth and bring the mixture to a boil. Reduce the heat to medium-low and cook, stirring occasionally, until the vegetables are tender, about 15 minutes.

4. Add the mushrooms, beans, peas, and cashews. Stir in the curry paste, soy sauce, and salt, and cook for 3 minutes.

5. Increase the heat to medium-high, bring to a boil, and gradually stir in the cornstarch mixture. Cook, stirring, until the stew is just thickened, about 1 minute.

6. Reduce the heat to low and cook, stirring occasionally, for 10 minutes to blend the flavors. Serve hot.

Spicy White Bean Chili

SERVES 4

◆ EXTRA-QUICK

2 TABLESPOONS OLIVE OIL

1 LARGE GREEN BELL PEPPER, COARSELY CHOPPED

1 SMALL FRESH OR PICKLED JALAPEÑO PEPPER, SEEDED AND MINCED

3 MEDIUM ONIONS, COARSELY CHOPPED

4 GARLIC CLOVES, MINCED

1 TABLESPOON HOT CHILI POWDER

ONE 16-OUNCE CAN NO-SALT-ADDED WHOLE TOMATOES

2 CUPS CANNED TOMATO PURÉE

½ CUP DRY RED WINE

1½ TEASPOONS OREGANO

1½ TEASPOONS CUMIN

1 BAY LEAF

PINCH OF SUGAR

TWO 16-OUNCE CANS WHITE KIDNEY BEANS (CANNELLINI), RINSED AND DRAINED

1. In a large saucepan, warm the oil over medium-high heat. Add the bell pepper, jalapeño, onions, garlic, and chili powder, and sauté, stirring frequently, until the vegetables are tender, about 4 minutes.

2. Add the tomatoes, breaking them up with the back of a spoon. Add the tomato purée, wine, oregano, cumin, bay leaf, and sugar. Reduce the heat to medium-low and simmer, stirring occasionally, for 20 minutes to blend the flavors.

3. Add the beans and simmer, stirring occasionally, until the chili is heated through, about 10 minutes.

4. Remove and discard the bay leaf. Ladle the chili into 4 shallow bowls and serve hot.

Chicken and Okra Gumbo with Confetti Rice

SERVES 4

4 CUPS REDUCED-SODIUM CHICKEN
BROTH

1 CUP RICE

2 TABLESPOONS UNSALTED BUTTER

½ CUP CHOPPED GREEN BELL PEPPER,
PLUS 2 TABLESPOONS MINCED

2 TABLESPOONS MINCED SCALLION

¾ TEASPOON SALT

½ CUP FLOUR

½ TEASPOON CAYENNE PEPPER

¼ TEASPOON BLACK PEPPER

2½ TO 3 POUNDS CHICKEN PARTS

2 TABLESPOONS VEGETABLE OIL

1 CELERY RIB, COARSELY CHOPPED

ONE 10-OUNCE PACKAGE FROZEN CUT
OKRA, THAWED

1 SMALL ONION, COARSELY CHOPPED

½ CUP CHOPPED RED BELL PEPPER

½ CUP CHOPPED GREEN BELL PEPPER

1 BAY LEAF

¼ POUND ANDOUILLE SAUSAGE OR
KIELBASA, DICED

1. Preheat the oven to 375°. In a medium saucepan, warm the broth until hot.

2. In a small casserole, combine 2 cups of the hot broth, the rice, 1 tablespoon of the butter, the minced green pepper, scallion, and ½ teaspoon of the salt. Cover and bake for 40 to 45 minutes, or until the rice is tender. Turn off the heat and keep rice warm in the oven.

3. Meanwhile, in a plastic or paper bag, combine the flour, cayenne, remaining ¼ teaspoon salt, and the black pepper. Add the chicken and shake to coat lightly.

4. In a large Dutch oven, warm the oil over medium-high heat. Add the chicken and cook until well browned, 5 to 7 minutes. Transfer the chicken to paper towels to drain.

5. Add the remaining 1 tablespoon butter to the pan. Add the celery, okra, onion, and chopped bell peppers. Cook, stirring, until the okra is tender, about 5 minutes.

6. Reheat the remaining 2 cups broth. Return the chicken to the casserole, add the hot broth and bay leaf, partially cover, and bring to a boil. Reduce the heat to low and simmer for 30 minutes. Uncover, stir in the sausage, and simmer for 10 minutes.

7. Remove and discard the bay leaf. Serve the gumbo hot over the rice.

POACHED CHICKEN AND VEGETABLES

SERVES 4

◆ EXTRA-QUICK

7 CUPS REDUCED-SODIUM CHICKEN
  BROTH
½ TEASPOON THYME
½ POUND SWEET ITALIAN SAUSAGE,
  CASINGS REMOVED
2½ TO 3 POUNDS CHICKEN PARTS
8 SMALL UNPEELED RED POTATOES,
  HALVED

3 MEDIUM CARROTS, CUT INTO 2-INCH
  LENGTHS
1 MEDIUM RED ONION, CUT INTO
  ½-INCH WEDGES
ONE 10-OUNCE PACKAGE FROZEN
  CORN KERNELS, THAWED

1. In a large saucepan or flameproof casserole, bring the broth and thyme to a boil over medium-high heat.

2. Add the sausage and chicken to the boiling broth. Reduce the heat to medium-low, cover, and simmer for 25 minutes, stirring occasionally to break up the sausage.

3. Increase the heat to medium-high and return the broth to a boil. Stir in the potatoes, carrots, and onion. Reduce the heat to medium-low, cover, and simmer until the potatoes are tender, about 15 minutes.

4. Add the corn to the mixture and cook until heated through, about 2 minutes.

5. To serve, divide the sausage, chicken, and vegetables among 4 shallow bowls, and spoon some of the broth on top of each.

Substitution: *Try making this one-pot dinner with hot, rather than sweet, Italian sausage. Or, to reduce the fat content of the dish, substitute turkey sausage for pork.*

Chicken Stew with Zucchini and Tomatoes

SERVES 4

◇ LOW-FAT

ONE 28-OUNCE CAN NO-SALT-ADDED
  WHOLE TOMATOES
1½ CUPS CHICKEN BROTH, PREFERABLY
  REDUCED-SODIUM
1 TEASPOON SUGAR
2 GARLIC CLOVES, FINELY CHOPPED
1 TEASPOON BASIL
¾ TEASPOON CHILI POWDER

½ TEASPOON SALT
¼ TEASPOON BLACK PEPPER
2 BONE-IN CHICKEN BREAST HALVES,
  SKINNED
3 OUNCES WIDE EGG NOODLES (ABOUT
  1½ CUPS)
2 MEDIUM ZUCCHINI, CUT INTO
  ½-INCH ROUNDS

1. In a large saucepan, combine the tomatoes, broth, sugar, garlic, basil, chili powder, salt, and pepper. Bring the mixture to a boil over medium-high heat, breaking up the tomatoes with the back of a spoon. Reduce the heat to medium-low and simmer, stirring occasionally, for 10 minutes.

2. Add the chicken breasts to the pan and simmer them for 12 minutes. With a slotted spoon, transfer the breasts (they will be slightly undercooked) to a plate. Remove the meat from the bones and cut the meat into ½-inch pieces.

3. Meanwhile, cook the noodles in a pot of boiling water for 3 minutes. Drain the noodles well, then add them to the stew along with the zucchini rounds and chicken. Cook until the zucchini is tender, about 5 minutes. Serve hot.

Coq au Vin

SERVES 4

¼ POUND BACON

2½ POUNDS CHICKEN PARTS

¼ CUP PLUS 3 TABLESPOONS FLOUR

1½ CUPS CHICKEN BROTH, PREFERABLY
    REDUCED-SODIUM

1½ CUPS DRY RED WINE

1 POUND SMALL UNPEELED RED
    POTATOES, HALVED

½ POUND SMALL MUSHROOMS

3 MEDIUM CARROTS, CUT INTO
    1½-INCH LENGTHS

2 CUPS FROZEN PEARL ONIONS, OR
    ½ POUND SMALL WHITE BOILING
    ONIONS, PEELED

3 GARLIC CLOVES, MINCED

1½ TEASPOONS THYME

½ TEASPOON SALT

¼ TEASPOON BLACK PEPPER

1 BAY LEAF

3 TABLESPOONS UNSALTED BUTTER, AT
    ROOM TEMPERATURE

1. In a flameproof casserole or large Dutch oven, cook the bacon over medium heat until crisp, about 10 minutes. Transfer the bacon to paper towels to drain; crumble and set aside.

2. Meanwhile, lightly dredge the chicken in ¼ cup of the flour; shake off any excess.

3. Add the chicken to the bacon drippings in the casserole and sauté over medium heat until golden, about 8 minutes per side.

4. Increase the heat to medium-high and add the broth, wine, potatoes, mushrooms, carrots, onions, garlic, thyme, salt, pepper, and bay leaf, and bring to a boil. Reduce the heat to low, cover, and simmer, stirring occasion-ally, until the potatoes and carrots are tender and the chicken is cooked through, about 30 minutes.

5. Blend the butter with the remaining 3 tablespoons flour. Return the stew to a boil over medium-high heat. Pinch off several pieces of the butter-flour mixture at a time, add them to the simmering stew, and stir well. Repeat until all of the mixture has been incorporated. Cook, stirring occasionally, until the sauce has thickened slightly, 2 to 3 minutes.

6. Discard the bay leaf. Stir in the crumbled bacon and serve hot.

Southwestern Chicken Stew

SERVES 4

2½ POUNDS CHICKEN PARTS

1 TABLESPOON OLIVE OIL

2 MEDIUM ONIONS, SLICED

5 GARLIC CLOVES, MINCED

2 TABLESPOONS FLOUR

3 TABLESPOONS CHILI POWDER

ONE 28-OUNCE CAN NO-SALT-ADDED
WHOLE TOMATOES

ONE 4-OUNCE CAN CHOPPED MILD
GREEN CHILIES, DRAINED

¾ TEASPOON SALT

¼ TEASPOON BLACK PEPPER

ONE 10-OUNCE PACKAGE FROZEN
CORN KERNELS

1. If you are using chicken breasts, cut them crosswise in half.

2. In a large skillet or flameproof casserole, warm the oil over medium-high heat. Add the chicken and cook until golden on all sides, 5 to 10 minutes. Transfer the chicken to a plate and set aside.

3. Add the onions and garlic, and cook, stirring frequently, until the onions are softened but not browned, about 5 minutes.

4. Stir in the flour and chili powder, and cook, stirring constantly, until the flour is no longer visible, about 30 seconds.

5. Stir in the tomatoes, breaking them up with the back of a spoon. Add the chilies, salt, and pepper. Return the chicken to the pan and bring the mixture to a boil. Reduce the heat to medium-low, cover, and simmer the stew, stirring occasionally, until the chicken is cooked through, about 20 minutes.

6. Stir in the corn and cook until heated through, about 5 minutes. Serve hot.

CHICKEN MARENGO

SERVES 4

1 TABLESPOON VEGETABLE OIL

2½ POUNDS CHICKEN PARTS

½ POUND SMALL WHITE BOILING
ONIONS, PEELED

3 GARLIC CLOVES, MINCED

TWO 16-OUNCE CANS CRUSHED
TOMATOES

ONE 12-OUNCE BOTTLE DARK BEER

½ CUP ORANGE JUICE

2 TABLESPOONS TOMATO PASTE

1 TABLESPOON GRATED ORANGE ZEST
(OPTIONAL)

¾ TEASPOON SALT

½ TEASPOON BLACK PEPPER

¾ POUND SMALL MUSHROOMS

3 LARGE CARROTS, CUT INTO 1½-INCH
CHUNKS

2 LARGE GREEN BELL PEPPERS, CUT
INTO STRIPS

1. In a large Dutch oven or flameproof casserole, warm the oil over medium-high heat. Add the chicken and brown well on all sides, about 20 minutes. Transfer to a plate and set aside.

2. Add the whole onions and garlic to the pan, and sauté until the onions begin to brown, about 5 minutes.

3. Add the tomatoes, beer, orange juice, tomato paste, orange zest (if using), salt, and black pepper, and bring the mixture to a boil. Add the mushrooms. Return the chicken to the pan, return to a boil, and reduce the heat to medium-low. Cover and simmer for 30 minutes, turning the chicken occasionally.

4. Stir in the carrots and bell peppers, cover, and cook, stirring occasionally, until the carrots are crisp-tender, about 15 minutes. Serve the stew hot.

KITCHEN NOTE: *If it suits your schedule, prepare this delicious stew a day in advance and refrigerate it overnight. This allows the flavors to mingle and mellow, and the extra time allows the sauce to permeate the chicken more thoroughly. Refrigerating the dish overnight also lets you easily skim any fat that congeals on top.*

Lentil and Smoked Turkey Stew with Tomatoes

SERVES 4

◇ LOW-FAT

1 TABLESPOON VEGETABLE OIL

1 LARGE ONION, COARSELY CHOPPED

3 GARLIC CLOVES, MINCED

1 CUP LENTILS, RINSED AND PICKED OVER

Two 14½-OUNCE CANS NO-SALT-ADDED STEWED TOMATOES

½ CUP CHICKEN BROTH, PREFERABLY REDUCED-SODIUM

½ CUP DRY RED WINE OR CHICKEN BROTH

1½ TEASPOONS THYME

¼ TEASPOON SUGAR

¼ TEASPOON BLACK PEPPER

1 BAY LEAF

¾ POUND SMOKED TURKEY, CUT INTO ½-INCH CUBES

¼ CUP CHOPPED PARSLEY (OPTIONAL)

1. In a large saucepan, warm the oil over medium-high heat. Add the onion and garlic, and stir-fry until the mixture begins to brown, 3 to 5 minutes.

2. Add the lentils, stewed tomatoes, broth, wine, thyme, sugar, pepper, and bay leaf, and bring to a boil. Reduce the heat to low, cover, and simmer, stirring occasionally, until the lentils are tender, about 40 minutes.

3. When the lentils are done, remove and discard the bay leaf. Transfer about 1 cup of the lentils to a food processor or blender and purée until smooth.

4. Return the lentil purée to the saucepan and add the turkey and parsley (if using). Cook over medium-high heat until the turkey is heated through, about 3 minutes. Serve hot.

SAVORY LENTIL STEW

SERVES 4

1 CUP LENTILS, RINSED AND PICKED OVER

3½ CUPS REDUCED-SODIUM CHICKEN BROTH

2 TEASPOONS THYME

½ TEASPOON SALT

¼ TEASPOON BLACK PEPPER

1 BAY LEAF

TWO 1 x ½-INCH STRIPS ORANGE ZEST

4 LARGE LINK SAUSAGES (ABOUT ¾ POUND TOTAL)

2 POUNDS CHICKEN THIGHS

3 LARGE CARROTS, CUT INTO MATCHSTICKS

4 MEDIUM CELERY RIBS, CHOPPED

2 MEDIUM ONIONS, CHOPPED

2 GARLIC CLOVES, LIGHTLY CRUSHED AND PEELED

1 CUP DRY WHITE WINE

1. In a large saucepan, combine the lentils, broth, thyme, salt, pepper, bay leaf, and orange zest. Bring the mixture to a boil over high heat. Reduce the heat to low, cover, and simmer until the lentils are just tender, 30 to 35 minutes.

2. Meanwhile, prick the sausages with a sharp knife. Place in a large skillet and cook, turning frequently, over medium-high heat until browned, about 5 minutes. Transfer to the paper towels to drain.

3. In the same skillet, cook the chicken over medium-high heat, turning occasionally, until browned on all sides, 6 to 8 minutes. Transfer to paper towels to drain.

4. Add the carrots and celery to the skillet, and sauté, stirring, over medium-high heat until softened, 3 to 4 minutes. Add the onions and garlic, and sauté until the onions are translucent, 3 to 4 minutes. Transfer the sautéed vegetables to the pan with lentils.

5. Drain off any drippings in the skillet. Add the wine and bring to a boil over high heat, stirring to scrape up any browned bits clinging to the bottom of the pan. Cook until the wine is slightly reduced, 2 to 3 minutes.

6. Add the reduced wine to the lentils. Arrange the chicken and sausages on top, cover, and simmer over medium-low heat for 30 minutes. Remove and discard the bay leaf. Serve the stew hot.

Cajun-Style Shrimp Stew

SERVES 4

1½ POUNDS MEDIUM SHRIMP, SHELLED
  AND DEVEINED, SHELLS RESERVED
4 PARSLEY SPRIGS
1 BAY LEAF
¾ TEASPOON SALT
¼ CUP VEGETABLE OIL
5 TABLESPOONS FLOUR
1 LARGE ONION, FINELY DICED

1 GARLIC CLOVE, MINCED
¼ CUP DICED GREEN BELL PEPPER
2 TABLESPOONS WORCESTERSHIRE
  SAUCE
1½ TEASPOONS HOT PEPPER SAUCE
1 CUP RICE
¼ CUP MINCED PARSLEY

1. In a medium saucepan, combine the shrimp shells, parsley sprigs, bay leaf, ¼ teaspoon of the salt, and 3½ cups of water, and bring to a boil over high heat. Reduce the heat to medium and simmer until the liquid is reduced to about 2½ cups, 8 to 10 minutes. Strain the shrimp broth through a sieve; set aside.

2. In a large skillet, warm the oil over medium heat. Stir in the flour and cook, stirring constantly, until the mixture turns a rich chocolate color, about 15 minutes.

3. Add the onion and garlic to the flour mixture, and cook, stirring constantly, for 3 minutes. Add the bell pepper and cook, stirring, for 2 minutes.

4. Gradually add the shrimp broth to the vegetable mixture and bring to a boil, stirring until the sauce is smooth. Stir in the Worcestershire sauce, hot pepper sauce, and ¼ teaspoon of the salt. Reduce the heat to low, cover, and simmer while you cook the rice.

5. Meanwhile, in a medium saucepan, bring 2 cups of water to a boil over high heat. Stir in the rice and remaining ¼ teaspoon salt; cover, reduce the heat to low, and simmer until the rice is tender, 15 to 20 minutes.

6. Stir the shrimp into the simmering broth mixture and cook until the shrimp are just firm, 2 to 3 minutes. Sprinkle the stew with the minced parsley and serve over the rice.

SEAFOOD STEW

SERVES 4

¼ CUP OLIVE OIL

1 MEDIUM ONION, COARSELY CHOPPED

8 MUSHROOMS, VERY THINLY SLICED

2 GARLIC CLOVES, LIGHTLY CRUSHED
  AND PEELED

ONE 16-OUNCE CAN NO-SALT-ADDED
  WHOLE TOMATOES

ONE 8-OUNCE BOTTLE CLAM JUICE OR
  1 CUP CHICKEN BROTH

1 CUP DRY WHITE WINE

½ TEASPOON BASIL

⅛ TEASPOON FENNEL SEEDS

⅛ TEASPOON SAFFRON THREADS OR
  TURMERIC

⅛ TEASPOON WHITE PEPPER

2 POUNDS LITTLENECK CLAMS

½ POUND MONKFISH OR COD FILLETS,
  CUT INTO BITE-SIZE PIECES

½ POUND SALMON FILLETS, WITH SKIN

6 OUNCES LUMP CRABMEAT OR MEDIUM
  SHRIMP, SHELLED AND DEVEINED

1. In a large saucepan, warm the oil over medium heat. Add the onion and cook, stirring frequently, until softened but not browned, about 5 minutes.

2. Add the mushrooms and garlic, and cook, stirring, until softened, about 3 minutes.

3. Add the tomatoes, breaking them up with the back of a spoon. Stir in the clam juice, wine, basil, fennel seeds, saffron, and pepper. Bring to a boil over high heat. Reduce the heat to low, cover, and simmer for 30 minutes to blend the flavors.

4. Add the clams, cover, and simmer for 5 minutes. Add the fish and crab, cover, and simmer until the clam shells open, about 10 minutes. Discard any clams that have not opened.

5. Ladle the stew into a tureen or divide among 4 individual bowls and serve hot.

Italian-Style Veal Stew

SERVES 4

¼ CUP FLOUR

½ TEASPOON SALT

½ TEASPOON BLACK PEPPER

1½ POUNDS STEW VEAL, CUT INTO
1½-INCH CHUNKS

1 TABLESPOON OLIVE OIL

1 TABLESPOON UNSALTED BUTTER

ONE 14½-OUNCE CAN NO-SALT-ADDED
STEWED TOMATOES

1 CUP DRY RED WINE OR BEEF BROTH

1½ TEASPOONS THYME

1 BAY LEAF

2 MEDIUM CARROTS, CUT INTO
½-INCH SLICES

¼ POUND SMALL MUSHROOMS, HALVED

1 LARGE GREEN BELL PEPPER, CUT INTO
THIN STRIPS

½ CUP STUFFED GREEN OLIVES

1. In a plastic or paper bag, combine the flour, salt, and pepper, and shake to mix. Add the veal and shake to coat lightly. Remove the veal and reserve the excess seasoned flour.

2. In a large skillet, warm the oil with the butter over medium-high heat until the butter is melted. Add the veal and cook until browned all over, about 10 minutes.

3. Stir the reserved seasoned flour into the skillet and cook, stirring, until the flour is no longer visible, about 30 seconds.

4. Add the stewed tomatoes, wine, thyme, and bay leaf. Bring the mixture to a boil over medium-high heat. Add the carrots and mushrooms, and return to a boil. Reduce the heat to low, cover, and simmer until the veal is tender, about 20 minutes.

5. Add the bell pepper and olives, and simmer until the flavors have blended and the pepper is tender, about 8 minutes.

6. Remove and discard the bay leaf. Serve the veal stew hot.

BEEF CHILI WITH CHEESE

SERVES 4

1 TABLESPOON VEGETABLE OIL

1½ POUNDS LEAN GROUND BEEF

2 MEDIUM ONIONS, CHOPPED

ONE 35-OUNCE CAN NO-SALT-ADDED
WHOLE TOMATOES

6 TABLESPOONS TOMATO PASTE

ONE 15-OUNCE CAN RED KIDNEY
BEANS, RINSED AND DRAINED

2 TABLESPOONS CHILI POWDER

½ TEASPOON SALT

½ TEASPOON BLACK PEPPER

HOT PEPPER SAUCE

1 CUP SHREDDED CHEDDAR CHEESE

1. In a Dutch oven or flameproof casserole, warm the oil over medium-high heat. Add the beef and sauté, stirring to break up the meat, until browned, 3 to 4 minutes.

2. Drain off the fat and excess oil from the pan. Increase the heat to high, add the onions, and cook, stirring frequently, until translucent, 3 to 5 minutes.

3. Stir in the tomatoes and bring to a boil, breaking up the tomatoes with the back of a spoon. Add the tomato paste and stir until blended. Reduce the heat to low and simmer gently, stirring occasionally, for 20 minutes.

4. Add the kidney beans, chili powder, salt, pepper, and hot pepper sauce, to taste. Stir well to combine and simmer the mixture for 20 minutes.

5. Turn the chili into a large bowl, sprinkle with the Cheddar, and serve.

VARIATION: *Chili can be made with just about any kind of meat—or no meat at all. For a change, make this one with ground pork loin, ground turkey, or even ground lamb. Offer toppings alongside: sour cream, chopped scallions, and minced cilantro.*

CHUNKY BEEF STEW WITH OLIVES

SERVES 4

¼ CUP FLOUR

¼ TEASPOON BLACK PEPPER

1 POUND STEW BEEF, CUT INTO
   1-INCH CUBES

1 TABLESPOON OLIVE OIL

1 MEDIUM ONION, COARSELY CHOPPED

3 GARLIC CLOVES, MINCED

ONE 16-OUNCE CAN NO-SALT-ADDED
   WHOLE TOMATOES

1 CUP BEEF BROTH

¾ CUP RED WINE OR BEEF BROTH

1½ TEASPOONS OREGANO

1 BAY LEAF

ONE 10-OUNCE PACKAGE FROZEN LIMA
   BEANS

1 CUP PITTED BLACK OLIVES

1. In a plastic or paper bag, combine the flour and pepper, and shake to mix. Add the beef and shake to coat lightly. Remove the beef.

2. In a large skillet, warm the oil over medium-high heat. Add the beef and cook, stirring frequently, until browned all over, about 10 minutes.

3. Add the onion and garlic, and cook, stirring, for 1 minute. Add the tomatoes, breaking them up with the back of a spoon. Stir in the broth, wine, oregano, and bay leaf, and

bring the liquid to a boil. Reduce the heat to low, cover, and simmer, stirring occasionally, until the beef is tender, about 20 minutes.

4. Add the lima beans and olives, increase the heat to medium-high, cover, and return the mixture to a boil. Reduce the heat to medium-low and simmer until the lima beans are heated through, about 5 minutes.

GREEK LAMB STEW WITH PASTA

SERVES 4 TO 6

¼ CUP FLOUR

½ TEASPOON SALT

¼ TEASPOON BLACK PEPPER

1 POUND STEW LAMB, CUT INTO
   1½-INCH CUBES

3 TABLESPOONS OLIVE OIL

1 MEDIUM ONION, COARSELY CHOPPED

3 GARLIC CLOVES, MINCED

TWO 14½-OUNCE CANS NO-SALT-
   ADDED STEWED TOMATOES

¼ CUP PITTED BLACK OLIVES, FINELY
   CHOPPED

2 TABLESPOONS TOMATO PASTE

1½ TEASPOONS OREGANO

1½ TEASPOONS THYME

PINCH OF SUGAR

1 BAY LEAF

½ POUND ORZO

1½ TEASPOONS GRATED LEMON ZEST

1. In a plastic or paper bag, combine the flour, salt, and pepper, and shake to mix. Add the lamb and shake to coat lightly. Remove the lamb and reserve the excess seasoned flour.

2. In a large skillet, warm 2 tablespoons of the oil over medium-high heat. Add the lamb and cook until browned on all sides, about 10 minutes. Transfer the lamb to a plate and cover loosely with foil to keep warm.

3. Add the remaining 1 tablespoon oil to the skillet, and warm over medium-high heat. Add the onion and garlic, and cook, stirring frequently, for 1 minute. Stir in the reserved seasoned flour and cook, stirring, until the flour is no longer visible, about 30 seconds.

4. Add the tomatoes, olives, tomato paste, oregano, thyme, sugar, and bay leaf. Return the lamb to the skillet and bring to a boil. Reduce the heat to low, cover, and simmer until the lamb is tender, about 45 minutes.

5. About 20 minutes before the stew is done, bring a large pot of water to a boil. Add the orzo and cook until al dente according to package directions. Drain well.

6. Stir the lemon zest into the stew; remove and discard the bay leaf. Serve the stew with the orzo.

EASY IRISH STEW

SERVES 4

♦ EXTRA-QUICK   ◇ LOW-FAT

2¾ CUPS BEEF BROTH

¼ CUP TOMATO PASTE

3 GARLIC CLOVES, MINCED

1 BAY LEAF

¼ TEASPOON BLACK PEPPER

1 CUP FROZEN PEARL ONIONS

1 POUND STEW LAMB, CUT INTO BITE-
SIZE PIECES

1 POUND SMALL UNPEELED RED
POTATOES, QUARTERED

3 LARGE CARROTS, CUT INTO 2-INCH
PIECES

2 TABLESPOONS CORNSTARCH

1 CUP FROZEN PEAS

1. In a large saucepan, combine 2½ cups of the broth, the tomato paste, garlic, bay leaf, and pepper. Add the pearl onions and bring the mixture to a boil over medium-high heat.

2. Add the lamb, potatoes, and carrots, and return to a boil. Reduce the heat to medium-low, cover, and simmer until the vegetables are tender, about 20 minutes.

3. In a small bowl, combine the remaining ¼ cup broth with the cornstarch, and stir to blend. Increase the heat under the stew to medium-high and return to a boil. Stir in the cornstarch mixture and peas. Cook, stirring constantly, until the peas are heated through and the stew thickens, about 1 minute.

4. Remove and discard the bay leaf, and serve the stew hot.

SWEET AFTERTHOUGHT: *While the kids enjoy their favorite dessert, treat the grownups to steaming mugs of Irish coffee. For each serving, pour a jigger of Irish whiskey into a mug and add 1 to 2 teaspoons sugar. Fill the mugs with strong, hot coffee, leaving a little room at the top for a big dollop of sweetened whipped cream.*

VEGETABLE JAMBALAYA

SERVES 4

◆ EXTRA-QUICK

3 TABLESPOONS UNSALTED BUTTER

2 MEDIUM ONIONS, CHOPPED

3 MEDIUM GARLIC CLOVES, MINCED

1 LARGE GREEN BELL PEPPER, COARSELY
   CHOPPED

1 LARGE RED BELL PEPPER, COARSELY
   CHOPPED

1½ CUPS CHOPPED CELERY

2 CUPS CHICKEN BROTH, PREFERABLY
   REDUCED-SODIUM

ONE 16-OUNCE CAN NO-SALT-ADDED
   WHOLE TOMATOES

3 BAY LEAVES

1 TABLESPOON HOT PEPPER SAUCE

1 TEASPOON HOT PAPRIKA

1 TEASPOON THYME

1 TEASPOON OREGANO

½ TEASPOON CAYENNE PEPPER

½ TEASPOON BLACK PEPPER

¾ TEASPOON SALT

1½ CUPS RICE

1 CUP BLANCHED OR RAW PEANUTS

1 CUP CHOPPED SCALLIONS

1½ CUPS SLICED OKRA, FRESH OR
   FROZEN

1. In a large flameproof casserole, warm the butter over medium-high heat until melted. Add the onions, garlic, bell peppers, and celery, and sauté, stirring frequently, until the vegetables begin to soften, about 5 minutes.

2. Add the broth, tomatoes, bay leaves, hot pepper sauce, paprika, thyme, oregano, cayenne, black pepper, and salt, and break up the tomatoes with the back of a spoon. Bring the mixture to a boil, stirring frequently. Partially cover the pan, reduce the heat to medium-low, and simmer for 5 minutes.

3. Stir in the rice and peanuts, and simmer, partially covered, for 10 minutes.

4. Stir in the scallions and okra, and simmer, partially covered, until the rice is tender, about 10 minutes.

5. Remove and discard the bay leaves. Serve the jambalaya hot.

Mushroom and Pepper Frittata

SERVES 4

◆ EXTRA - QUICK

¼ CUP CHICKEN BROTH

1 TEASPOON THYME

1 LARGE RED BELL PEPPER, CUT INTO
  THIN STRIPS

8 SCALLIONS, COARSELY CHOPPED

½ POUND SMALL MUSHROOMS,
  QUARTERED

3 WHOLE EGGS

2 EGG WHITES

¼ TEASPOON SALT

¼ TEASPOON BLACK PEPPER

1 TABLESPOON UNSALTED BUTTER

1. In a medium saucepan, bring the broth and ½ teaspoon of the thyme to a boil over medium-high heat. Add the bell pepper, scallions, and mushrooms. Reduce the heat to medium-low, cover, and simmer, stirring occasionally, until the bell pepper is crisp-tender, about 5 minutes.

2. Uncover the vegetables, increase the heat to medium, and boil off any liquid remaining in the saucepan, 3 to 5 minutes.

3. Meanwhile, in a bowl, beat the whole eggs and egg whites together with the remaining ½ teaspoon thyme, the salt, and black pepper.

4. Preheat the broiler.

5. In a medium broilerproof skillet, warm the butter over medium-high heat until melted. Add the vegetables and the egg mixture, and spread evenly in the pan. Reduce the heat to medium, cover, and cook until the mixture is almost set, 7 to 10 minutes.

6. Place the skillet under the broiler for 5 minutes, or until the frittata is set and the top is browned.

7. To serve, cut the frittata into pie-shaped wedges.

Kitchen Note: *A frittata, the Italian version of an omelet, is easy to make and wonderfully versatile: You can "fill" it with all sorts of vegetables and/or cheese, poultry, or meat. It's an especially good way to use leftovers, even leftover pasta or rice.*

Stovetop Chicken with Spanish Rice

SERVES 4

◆ EXTRA-QUICK

2 TABLESPOONS OLIVE OIL

2½ POUNDS CHICKEN PARTS

1 MEDIUM ONION, THINLY SLICED

1 LARGE GREEN BELL PEPPER, CUT INTO
THIN STRIPS

2 GARLIC CLOVES, MINCED

1 CUP RICE

ONE 16-OUNCE CAN NO-SALT-ADDED
WHOLE TOMATOES

1¾ CUPS CHICKEN BROTH, PREFERABLY
REDUCED-SODIUM

1 BAY LEAF

2 TEASPOONS PAPRIKA

¼ TEASPOON BLACK PEPPER

½ CUP PITTED BLACK OR PIMIENTO-
STUFFED GREEN OLIVES

1. In a flameproof casserole or Dutch oven, warm 1 tablespoon of the oil over medium-high heat. Add the chicken and cook until browned all over, about 10 minutes. Transfer the chicken to a plate and set aside.

2. Add the remaining 1 tablespoon oil to the casserole. Add the onion, bell pepper, and garlic, and cook, stirring frequently, until the onion is translucent, about 5 minutes.

3. Add the rice and cook, stirring constantly to coat with the oil, for 2 minutes. Add the tomatoes, broth, bay leaf, paprika, and black pepper, and break up the tomatoes with the back of a spoon.

4. Return the chicken to the pan. Bring the mixture to a boil, reduce the heat to medium-low, cover, and simmer, stirring occasionally, until the chicken is cooked through, about 20 minutes.

5. Remove and discard the bay leaf. Stir in the olives and serve the chicken and rice hot.

CHICKEN WITH OLIVES

SERVES 4

¼ CUP OLIVE OIL

8 CHICKEN DRUMSTICKS (ABOUT 3 POUNDS TOTAL)

½ TEASPOON SALT

1 MEDIUM ONION, CUT INTO THIN RINGS

3 MEDIUM GARLIC CLOVES, MINCED

2 MEDIUM RED BELL PEPPERS, CUT INTO LARGE PIECES

1 TABLESPOON FLOUR

½ CUP DRY RED WINE

⅓ CUP CHICKEN BROTH

2 TABLESPOONS RED WINE VINEGAR

ONE 16-OUNCE CAN NO-SALT-ADDED WHOLE TOMATOES, DRAINED WITH 3 TABLESPOONS JUICE RESERVED

1 TABLESPOON MINCED FRESH OREGANO, OR 1 TEASPOON DRIED

1½ TEASPOONS FRESH THYME, OR ½ TEASPOON DRIED

⅛ TO ¼ TEASPOON RED PEPPER FLAKES

½ CUP PITTED BLACK OLIVES

½ CUP PITTED GREEN OLIVES

4 FLAT ANCHOVY FILLETS—RINSED, DRAINED, AND MINCED (OPTIONAL)

1. In a large skillet, warm the oil over medium-high heat. Add the chicken and cook, turning once, until browned on all sides, 10 to 15 minutes. Transfer the chicken to a plate and sprinkle with the salt.

2. Add the onion, garlic, and bell peppers to the pan, reduce the heat to medium, cover, and cook for 5 minutes.

3. Sprinkle the vegetables with the flour and cook, stirring, for 3 minutes. Add the wine, broth, vinegar, tomatoes and juice, oregano, thyme, and red pepper flakes, and break up the tomatoes with the back of a spoon. In-

crease the heat to high and bring the mixture to a boil. Return the chicken to the pan, reduce the heat to low, cover, and simmer for 20 minutes.

4. Stir in the olives and anchovies (if using), and cook, uncovered, until the juices run clear when the chicken is pierced with knife, 10 to 15 minutes.

5. Transfer the chicken, vegetables, and sauce to a platter and serve.

Chicken with Tomatoes and Pan-Fried Vermicelli

SERVES 4

♦ EXTRA-QUICK

4 CUPS REDUCED-SODIUM CHICKEN
  BROTH
¾ POUND SKINLESS, BONELESS
  CHICKEN BREASTS
3 TABLESPOONS VEGETABLE OIL
¾ POUND VERMICELLI, BROKEN INTO
  3-INCH LENGTHS
1 MEDIUM ONION, FINELY CHOPPED

2 LARGE GARLIC CLOVES, MINCED
1 TEASPOON CUMIN
¼ TEASPOON CAYENNE PEPPER
¾ POUND TOMATOES, CHOPPED
1 LARGE GREEN BELL PEPPER, DICED
¼ TEASPOON SALT
½ CUP GRATED PARMESAN CHEESE
2 TABLESPOONS MINCED CILANTRO

1. In a medium saucepan, bring the broth to a boil over medium-high heat.

2. Add the chicken breasts to the boiling broth, reduce the heat to low, and simmer until the chicken is just cooked through, about 10 minutes. Transfer the chicken to a plate and cool slightly; reserve the broth.

3. Meanwhile, in a large skillet, warm 2 tablespoons of the oil over medium heat. Add the vermicelli and cook, stirring frequently, until browned, about 2 minutes. Transfer the vermicelli to a plate and set aside.

4. Add the remaining 1 tablespoon oil to the skillet. Add the onion and garlic, and cook, stirring frequently, until the onion is translucent, 2 to 3 minutes.

5. Meanwhile, coarsely shred the chicken.

6. Return the vermicelli to the pan and add the reserved broth. Stir in the cumin and cayenne, cover, and cook over medium heat for 4 minutes. Stir in the shredded chicken, tomatoes, and bell pepper. Cover and cook until the liquid is absorbed and the vermicelli is tender, about 4 minutes.

7. Season with the salt and transfer the mixture to a large serving dish. Sprinkle with 1 tablespoon of the Parmesan and the cilantro. Serve with the remaining Parmesan on the side.

Chicken and Vegetables with Capellini

SERVES 4

2 TABLESPOONS OLIVE OIL

4 SKINLESS, BONELESS CHICKEN
BREASTS, CUT INTO 3 X ½-INCH
STRIPS

1 SMALL ZUCCHINI, THINLY SLICED

1½ CUPS THINLY SLICED MUSHROOMS

1 LARGE ONION, CHOPPED

2½ CUPS CHOPPED NO-SALT-ADDED
CANNED TOMATOES

¾ CUP CHICKEN BROTH

2 TEASPOONS MINCED GARLIC

1 TABLESPOON CHOPPED FRESH BASIL,
OR ½ TEASPOON DRIED

¼ TEASPOON SALT

¼ TEASPOON WHITE PEPPER

½ POUND CAPELLINI OR VERMICELLI

1. In a large skillet, warm the oil over medium-high heat. Add the chicken and sauté, stirring frequently, until browned, about 4 minutes.

2. Add the zucchini, mushrooms, and onion, and sauté until the vegetables are slightly softened, 2 to 3 minutes.

3. Add the tomatoes, broth, garlic, basil, salt, and pepper, and stir to combine. Reduce the heat to medium-low, cover, and simmer until the chicken and vegetables are fork-tender, about 15 minutes.

4. Meanwhile, in a large pot of boiling water, cook the pasta until al dente according to package directions.

5. Drain the pasta and transfer it to a serving platter. Spoon the chicken and vegetables on top and serve hot.

Substitution: *The finest of pasta strands, capellini is also called capelli d'angelo—angel hair. Any other pasta strand or ribbon, such as spaghettini, perciatelli (a thick, hollow spaghetti), fettuccine, or linguine would be fine for this dish.*

ARROZ CON POLLO

SERVES 4

◇ LOW-FAT

3 TABLESPOONS OLIVE OIL

3 GARLIC CLOVES, MINCED

1 MEDIUM ONION, COARSELY CHOPPED

1 POUND SKINLESS, BONELESS CHICKEN
BREASTS, CUT INTO 1-INCH PIECES

1 CUP RICE

1 TABLESPOON PAPRIKA

1½ TEASPOONS THYME

¼ TEASPOON BLACK PEPPER

2 CUPS CHICKEN BROTH, PREFERABLY
REDUCED-SODIUM

¼ CUP DRY WHITE WINE OR CHICKEN
BROTH

3 PLUM TOMATOES OR 4 WHOLE
NO-SALT-ADDED CANNED TOMATOES,
COARSELY CHOPPED

½ TEASPOON SALT

PINCH OF CAYENNE PEPPER

1 BAY LEAF

1 LARGE GREEN BELL PEPPER, CUT INTO
THIN STRIPS

2 TABLESPOONS CHOPPED PIMIENTO
(OPTIONAL)

1 CUP FROZEN PEAS

1. In a large skillet, warm 2 tablespoons of the oil over medium-high heat. Add the garlic, onion, and chicken, and sauté, stirring frequently, until the onion begins to brown, about 10 minutes. Transfer the chicken mixture to a plate and set aside.

2. Add the remaining 1 tablespoon oil to the pan. Add the rice, paprika, thyme, and black pepper, and cook, stirring constantly to lightly coat the rice with the oil and spices, about 1 minute.

3. Add the broth, wine, tomatoes, salt, cayenne, and bay leaf. Bring the mixture to a boil. Add the bell pepper and pimiento (if using), and return to a boil. Reduce the heat to low, cover, and simmer until the rice is tender, about 20 minutes.

4. Stir in the peas. Return the chicken and onion mixture to the skillet, cover, and cook until the chicken is cooked through, about 3 minutes. Remove and discard the bay leaf before serving.

Mini Cassoulet

SERVES 4

1 TEASPOON VEGETABLE OIL

ONE 1½-POUND CORNISH HEN,
QUARTERED, OR 1½ POUNDS
CHICKEN PARTS

½ POUND COUNTRY PORK SAUSAGE,
CASINGS REMOVED

1 MEDIUM ONION, THINLY SLICED

3 GARLIC CLOVES, MINCED

2 TABLESPOONS FLOUR

2 CUPS CHICKEN BROTH, PREFERABLY
REDUCED-SODIUM

1½ TEASPOONS THYME

¼ TEASPOON BLACK PEPPER

1 BAY LEAF

3 MEDIUM CARROTS, CUT INTO 1-INCH
LENGTHS

ONE 19-OUNCE CAN WHITE KIDNEY
BEANS, RINSED AND DRAINED

ONE 19-OUNCE CAN RED KIDNEY
BEANS, RINSED AND DRAINED

1. In a large skillet, warm the oil over medium heat. Add the Cornish hen quarters and cook until browned all over, about 20 minutes. Transfer the hen to a plate and cover loosely with foil to keep warm.

2. Crumble the sausage into the skillet and cook, stirring frequently, until browned, about 5 minutes.

3. Add the onion and garlic, and cook, stirring frequently, until the onion begins to brown, about 5 minutes. Stir in the flour and cook, stirring constantly, until the flour is no longer visible, about 30 seconds.

4. Return the Cornish hen to the skillet. Add the broth, thyme, pepper, bay leaf, and car-rots. Bring to a boil over medium-high heat. Reduce the heat to low, cover, and simmer for 10 minutes.

5. Meanwhile, add about half the white and red kidney beans to a food processor and coarsely purée.

6. Add the beans (puréed and whole) to the casserole, increase the heat to medium, cover, and cook until the hen is cooked through, about 10 minutes.

7. Remove and discard the bay leaf before serving.

FETTUCCINE WITH SCALLOPS AND BASIL

SERVES 4

¼ POUND SHALLOTS OR ONION, MINCED

2 GARLIC CLOVES, MINCED

½ CUP CHOPPED FRESH BASIL

1 CUP CHICKEN BROTH, PREFERABLY REDUCED-SODIUM

½ CUP DRY WHITE WINE

¼ TEASPOON BLACK PEPPER

1 POUND SEA SCALLOPS, HALVED IF LARGE

1 CUP HALF-AND-HALF

2 MEDIUM CARROTS, CUT INTO MATCHSTICKS

½ POUND FETTUCCINE OR LINGUINE

1. In a medium saucepan, combine the shallots, garlic, ¼ cup of the basil, the broth, wine, and pepper, and bring to a boil over medium-high heat. Add the scallops. When the broth returns to a boil, cover, reduce the heat to low, and simmer just until the scallops are opaque, 3 to 5 minutes. With a slotted spoon, transfer the scallops to a plate and cover loosely with foil to keep warm.

2. Return the broth to a boil over medium heat and boil, uncovered, until reduced to ½ cup, 25 to 30 minutes.

3. Stir in the half-and-half and return the mixture to a boil. Immediately reduce the heat to medium-low and cook until the liquid forms a thick sauce, about 5 minutes. Add the carrots and cook until the carrots are barely tender, about 5 minutes.

4. Meanwhile, in a large pot of boiling water, cook the pasta until al dente according to package directions.

5. Return the scallops to the sauce and stir in the remaining ¼ cup basil. Reduce the heat to low and cook, stirring gently, just until the scallops are heated through, about 1 minute.

6. Drain the pasta, divide it among 4 plates and spoon the scallops and sauce on top.

Scampi with Quick Risotto

SERVES 4 TO 6

3 TABLESPOONS OLIVE OIL

1 LARGE ONION, CHOPPED

2 CUPS RICE

4 TABLESPOONS UNSALTED BUTTER

3½ TO 4 CUPS REDUCED-SODIUM
    CHICKEN BROTH

¾ TEASPOON SALT

¾ TEASPOON BLACK PEPPER

1¼ POUNDS LARGE SHRIMP, SHELLED
    AND DEVEINED

4 GARLIC CLOVES, MINCED

½ CUP DRY WHITE WINE

2 TEASPOONS FRESH LEMON JUICE

3 TABLESPOONS CHOPPED PARSLEY

3 TABLESPOONS FINE UNSEASONED DRY
    BREAD CRUMBS

1 CUP GRATED PARMESAN CHEESE

1. In a large saucepan, warm 1 tablespoon of the oil over medium-high heat. Add the onion and sauté until golden, about 5 minutes. Stir in the rice, 2 tablespoons of the butter, 3½ cups of the broth, and ½ teaspoon each of the salt and pepper. Reduce the heat to low, cover, and cook, stirring occasionally, for 10 minutes. If the rice sticks to the pan, add up to ½ cup of the remaining broth a bit at a time, stirring after each addition until incorporated.

2. Uncover the rice and allow any excess broth to boil off; or, if the rice seems dry, add some water. Cover and cook until the rice is tender and all the liquid is absorbed, 5 to 10 minutes. Remove the pan from the heat and keep covered until ready to serve.

3. Meanwhile, in a large nonstick skillet, warm the remaining 2 tablespoons oil over medium-high heat. Add the shrimp and sauté, stirring, until lightly golden, about 2 minutes. Add the garlic and sauté, stirring, until golden, about 3 minutes. Add the remaining 2 tablespoons butter, the wine, lemon juice, and the remaining ¼ teaspoon each salt and pepper. Cook until the shrimp are just opaque, about 5 minutes.

4. Sprinkle the shrimp with the parsley and bread crumbs, and cook for 1 minute.

5. Stir the Parmesan into the rice and transfer the rice to a serving platter. Spoon the shrimp on top and serve hot.

Stir-Fried Ginger Beef with Watercress

SERVES 4

One 2-inch piece fresh ginger, minced

1 teaspoon red pepper flakes

¼ cup dry sherry

¼ cup chicken broth

2 teaspoons cornstarch

1 teaspoon sugar

1 pound top round steak, cut into thin strips

2 medium cucumbers—halved lengthwise, seeded, and cut into very thin slices

¼ teaspoon salt

¼ cup rice wine vinegar or distilled white vinegar

1 teaspoon Oriental (dark) sesame oil

1 cup rice

1½ teaspoons vegetable oil, preferably peanut

1 bunch of watercress

1. In a large bowl, combine the ginger, red pepper flakes, sherry, broth, cornstarch, and sugar. Add the beef and toss well; cover the bowl and marinate the meat for 30 minutes at room temperature.

2. Meanwhile, in a medium bowl, combine the cucumbers, salt, vinegar, and sesame oil. Cover and refrigerate until serving time.

3. In a medium saucepan, combine the rice and 2 cups of water, and bring to a boil over medium-high heat. Reduce the heat to low, cover, and cook until the rice is tender and the liquid is absorbed, about 20 minutes.

4. Drain the beef, reserving the marinade. In a large nonstick skillet or wok, warm the vegetable oil over high heat. Add the beef and stir-fry until well browned, about 2 minutes. Add the reserved marinade and cook; stirring constantly until the sauce thickens, about 1 minute. Add the watercress and toss the mixture quickly.

5. Serve the stir-fried beef and watercress with the rice and chilled cucumber salad.

BEEF STIR-FRY
WITH WINTER VEGETABLES

SERVES 4

◆ EXTRA-QUICK

1¼ CUPS BEEF BROTH

1 SMALL ONION, THINLY SLICED

2 TURNIPS, QUARTERED AND CUT INTO
    ¼-INCH-THICK SLICES

2 TEASPOONS TARRAGON

¾ POUND BUTTERNUT SQUASH—
    PEELED, QUARTERED AND CUT INTO
    ¼-INCH-THICK SLICES

1 POUND BEEF TENDERLOIN, CUT INTO
    2-INCH-LONG STRIPS

¼ TEASPOON SALT

¼ TEASPOON BLACK PEPPER

1 TABLESPOON OLIVE OIL

1 GARLIC CLOVE, MINCED

1 TABLESPOON CORNSTARCH BLENDED
    WITH 1 TABLESPOON WATER

1 TEASPOON DISTILLED WHITE VINEGAR

1. Place the broth and the onion in a saucepan. Set a vegetable steamer in the pan and bring the broth to a simmer.

2. Put the turnips into the steamer, sprinkle with 1 teaspoon of the tarragon, cover, and steam for 2 minutes. Add the squash and the remaining 1 teaspoon tarragon, and steam the vegetables until they are tender, about 3 minutes. Transfer the vegetables to a plate and set aside; reserve the broth and onion.

3. Season the beef with the salt and pepper. In a large skillet, warm 1½ teaspoons of the oil over high heat. Add the beef and stir-fry

for 2 minutes. Transfer the meat to a plate and cover loosely with foil to keep warm.

4. Add the remaining 1½ teaspoons oil to the skillet. Add the garlic and the reserved vegetables, and stir-fry for 3 minutes. Add the beef, toss to combine, and push the ingredients to the sides of the skillet. Pour in the reserved broth and onions and bring them to a simmer. Whisk in the cornstarch mixture and the vinegar, and cook, whisking, until the liquid thickens, about 2 minutes.

5. Serve the beef and vegetables with the sauce.

Beef in Spicy Tomato Sauce with Black Beans

SERVES 6

4 TABLESPOONS OLIVE OIL

1 LARGE ONION, THINLY SLICED

1 LARGE RED BELL PEPPER, CUT INTO
   THIN STRIPS

2 GARLIC CLOVES, MINCED

ONE 6-OUNCE CAN TOMATO PASTE

2 TABLESPOONS CUMIN

1 TABLESPOON CHOPPED CILANTRO

1 TEASPOON HOT PEPPER SAUCE

1 CUP RICE

1 TABLESPOON CURRY POWDER

½ TEASPOON SALT

2 CUPS BOILING WATER

2 POUNDS BONELESS SIRLOIN STEAK,
   CUT INTO ⅛-INCH-THICK SLICES

ONE 16-OUNCE CAN BLACK BEANS,
   RINSED AND DRAINED

¼ CUP CHOPPED SCALLIONS

¼ CUP CHOPPED PARSLEY

1. In a medium saucepan, warm 1 tablespoon of the oil over medium heat. Add the onion, bell pepper, and garlic, and sauté, stirring frequently, for 1 minute. Stir in the tomato paste, cumin, cilantro, and hot pepper sauce, and cook, stirring, for 1 to 2 minutes. Stir in 2 cups of water, reduce the heat to low, and cook, stirring occasionally, for 45 minutes.

2. Half an hour before serving, in a medium skillet, warm 1 tablespoon of the oil over medium-high heat. Add the rice and sauté, stirring, for 30 seconds. Stir in the curry powder and salt, and sauté, stirring, for 30 seconds. Stir in the boiling water, reduce the heat to low, cover, and cook until the water is com-

pletely absorbed and the rice is tender, about 20 minutes.

3. Meanwhile, in a large nonstick skillet, warm the remaining 2 tablespoons oil over medium-high heat. Add the beef slices, in batches if necessary, and sauté just until very rare. (The beef will continue to cook when the sauce is added to it.) Add the warm sauce and toss quickly to combine. Add the black beans and toss again.

4. Fluff the rice with a fork and stir in the scallions and parsley. Spoon the rice into a serving bowl and top with the beef and bean mixture.

Orange-Fried
Beef and Snow Peas

SERVES 4

1 POUND BONELESS SIRLOIN STEAK,
    CUT INTO VERY THIN STRIPS
2 TEASPOONS GRATED LEMON ZEST
2 TABLESPOONS CORNSTARCH
1 TABLESPOON PLUS 1 TEASPOON
    SUGAR
2 ORANGES
1 TABLESPOON PLUS 1 TEASPOON
    VEGETABLE OIL

2 TEASPOONS SLIVERED FRESH GINGER
¼ TEASPOON SALT
⅛ TEASPOON CAYENNE PEPPER
3 TABLESPOONS RICE WINE VINEGAR OR
    DISTILLED WHITE VINEGAR
1 POUND SNOW PEAS

1. In a large bowl, combine the beef, lemon zest, cornstarch, and sugar. Mix well to coat the beef and set aside.

2. Pare the zest from the oranges with a sharp knife. Slice the zest into fine julienne (you should have about ½ cup) and reserve it. Squeeze the juice from the oranges and pour it into a small saucepan. Boil the juice over medium heat until only 3 tablespoons remain and set it aside.

3. In a large nonstick skillet or wok, warm 2 teaspoons of the oil over high heat. Add the orange zest and ginger, and cook, stirring constantly, for 1 minute. Transfer the zest-ginger mixture to a plate and set aside.

4. Add half of the beef to the hot pan, distributing it in a single layer. Stir-fry the beef until browned, 3 to 4 minutes. Transfer the cooked beef to a plate. Add the remaining 2 teaspoons oil to the pan and stir-fry the remaining meat. Return the already-cooked beef and the zest-ginger mixture to the pan. Add the salt and cayenne, then pour in the vinegar and reduced orange juice. Stir-fry the meat until all the liquid has evaporated, about 2 minutes.

5. Meanwhile, steam the snow peas until crisp-tender, about 2 minutes. Transfer the snow peas to a serving platter and mound the beef on top. Serve hot.

Chinese Pork and Rice Casserole

SERVES 4

2 TABLESPOONS ORIENTAL (DARK) SESAME OIL

4 QUARTER-SIZE SLICES FRESH GINGER, MINCED

3 GARLIC CLOVES, MINCED

4 SCALLIONS, COARSELY CHOPPED

¾ POUND LEAN GROUND PORK

1 CUP RICE

2 MEDIUM CARROTS, COARSELY CHOPPED

4 CUPS CHOPPED NAPA CABBAGE

½ POUND SMALL MUSHROOMS

1 CUP BEEF BROTH

2 TABLESPOONS REDUCED-SODIUM SOY SAUCE

2 TABLESPOONS CHOPPED PARSLEY (OPTIONAL)

1. In a large skillet, warm 1 tablespoon of the sesame oil over medium-high heat. Add the ginger, garlic, scallions, and ground pork, and stir-fry, breaking up the meat, until the pork is no longer pink, about 5 minutes.

2. Add the remaining 1 tablespoon oil and the rice to the pan. Reduce the heat to medium and cook, stirring constantly, until the rice is coated with the oil.

3. Add the carrots, cabbage, mushrooms, broth, 1 cup of water, and the soy sauce, and bring the mixture to a boil. Reduce the heat to low, cover, and simmer until the rice is tender, about 20 minutes. Stir in the parsley (if using), and serve hot.

Variation: *Fresh sprouts, available in the produce section of your supermarket, would add a pleasant crunchiness to this hearty dish. You may find delicate green alfalfa sprouts, spicy radish sprouts, and lentil or adzuki sprouts—sold individually or in combinations. Stir about 1 cup of sprouts into the rice mixture just before serving and cover the pan for a moment to barely wilt them.*

HAM AND TURKEY SKILLET RICE

SERVES 4

◆ EXTRA-QUICK

¼ POUND BACON

1 MEDIUM ONION, COARSELY CHOPPED

1 CUP RICE

ONE 28-OUNCE CAN NO-SALT-ADDED
 WHOLE TOMATOES

1 CUP CHICKEN BROTH, PREFERABLY
 REDUCED-SODIUM

½ TEASPOON THYME

¼ TEASPOON BLACK PEPPER

1 BAY LEAF

½ POUND COOKED TURKEY, CUT INTO
 ½-INCH CUBES

½ POUND LEAN HAM, CUT INTO
 ½-INCH CUBES

1 MEDIUM RED BELL PEPPER, SLIVERED

¼ CUP CHOPPED PARSLEY (OPTIONAL)

1. In a flameproof casserole or large skillet, cook the bacon over medium heat until crisp, about 10 minutes. Reserving the fat in the pan, drain the bacon on paper towels; crumble and set aside.

2. Add the onion and the rice to the pan, and cook, stirring constantly, for 2 minutes. Increase the heat to medium-high and add the tomatoes, broth, thyme, black pepper, and bay leaf. Bring the mixture to a boil, breaking up the tomatoes with the back of a spoon. Reduce the heat to medium-low, cover, and simmer for 15 minutes.

3. Stir the turkey, ham, and bell pepper into the skillet. Cover and cook, stirring occasionally, until the pepper is softened and the flavors are blended, about 5 minutes.

4. Remove and discard the bay leaf. Serve the rice mixture sprinkled with the bacon and parsley (if using).

Peasant-Style Risotto

SERVES 4

2 TABLESPOONS VEGETABLE OIL

2 MEDIUM CARROTS, COARSELY
   CHOPPED

2 MEDIUM ONIONS, COARSELY
   CHOPPED

1¼ POUNDS SWEET ITALIAN SAUSAGE,
   CUT INTO ¼-INCH-THICK SLICES

1 POUND CABBAGE, SHREDDED

3 CANNED WHOLE TOMATOES, DRAINED

1 LARGE GARLIC CLOVE, MINCED

2 BAY LEAVES

½ TEASPOON ROSEMARY

½ TEASPOON OREGANO

ABOUT 5 CUPS REDUCED-SODIUM
   CHICKEN OR BEEF BROTH

¾ CUP DRY RED WINE

1¼ CUPS ARBORIO RICE

ONE 15-OUNCE CAN PINTO BEANS,
   RINSED AND DRAINED

½ TEASPOON SALT

½ TEASPOON BLACK PEPPER

1. In a large saucepan, warm the oil over medium-high heat. Add the carrots, onions, and sausage, and cook, stirring frequently, until the onions are golden, 3 to 5 minutes.

2. Spoon off all but about ¼ cup of the fat from the saucepan, if necessary. Stir in the cabbage, tomatoes, garlic, bay leaves, rosemary, and oregano, and cook, stirring frequently, over medium-high heat, until fragrant, 3 to 4 minutes.

3. Meanwhile, in a medium saucepan, bring the broth to a boil over high heat. Reduce the heat and keep at a simmer.

4. Add the wine and rice to the vegetable-sausage mixture and bring to a boil, stirring to prevent the rice from sticking. Reduce the heat to medium and stir in 2 cups of the hot broth. Cover and cook, stirring occasionally, until the broth is absorbed and the mixture is creamy, about 10 minutes.

5. Add the beans and 2 cups of the hot broth to the rice and cook, stirring occasionally, until the rice is still a bit firm and the consistency is quite creamy. If the rice seems undercooked, or if the consistency is not creamy, add the remaining 1 cup broth. Remove from the heat, cover, and set aside to rest for about 15 minutes.

6. Remove the bay leaves. Season with the salt and pepper, and transfer to a serving bowl.

Sausage and Spinach Pilaf

SERVES 4

◆ EXTRA-QUICK

¾ POUND COUNTRY SAUSAGE, CASINGS
   REMOVED
1 MEDIUM RED ONION, COARSELY
   CHOPPED
1 LARGE YELLOW, RED, OR GREEN BELL
   PEPPER, COARSELY CHOPPED
1 CUP RICE

2 CUPS CHICKEN BROTH, PREFERABLY
   REDUCED-SODIUM
¼ TEASPOON BLACK PEPPER
ONE 10-OUNCE PACKAGE FROZEN
   SPINACH, THAWED
½ CUP GRATED PARMESAN CHEESE

1. In a large skillet, cook the sausage over medium heat for 5 minutes, breaking it up with a spoon.

2. Add the onion and cook until the sausage and onion begin to brown, about 5 minutes.

3. Add the bell pepper and rice, and cook, stirring, for about 1 minute to coat the rice with fat.

4. Add the chicken broth and black pepper, and bring to a boil over medium-high heat. Reduce the heat to low, cover, and simmer for 15 minutes.

5. Add the spinach and stir to evenly distribute it. Re-cover and cook for 15 minutes.

6. Stir in the Parmesan and serve hot.

KITCHEN NOTES: *An excellent make-ahead candidate, the pilaf can be prepared through Step 5, then transferred to a microwavable casserole and refrigerated. At serving time, add ¼ cup of broth or water and reheat in the microwave, then stir in the Parmesan. You can also save time by thawing the spinach in the microwave: Remove it from the package and place it on a plate; microwave on High for 3 minutes. Squeeze the spinach dry between paper towels.*

Moroccan Couscous

SERVES 6

3 MEDIUM ONIONS, CUT INTO ½-INCH
    WEDGES
3 MEDIUM ZUCCHINI, THINLY SLICED
4 MEDIUM CARROTS, THINLY SLICED
ONE 15-OUNCE CAN CHICK-PEAS,
    RINSED AND DRAINED
1 CUP GOLDEN RAISINS
4 TABLESPOONS UNSALTED BUTTER
½ TEASPOON GROUND GINGER
½ TEASPOON SALT

½ TEASPOON BLACK PEPPER
¼ TEASPOON CINNAMON
2 POUNDS BONELESS LEG OF LAMB,
    CUT INTO 1-INCH CUBES
2 CUPS CHICKEN BROTH, PREFERABLY
    REDUCED-SODIUM
2 CUPS COUSCOUS
1½ POUNDS TOMATOES, COARSELY
    CHOPPED
⅓ CUP CHOPPED PARSLEY

1. In a large bowl, combine the onions, zucchini, carrots, chick-peas, and raisins. Toss to mix well; set aside.

2. In a large skillet, warm 2 tablespoons of the butter over medium-high heat until melted. Add the ginger, salt, pepper, and cinnamon, and cook, stirring constantly, for 1 minute. Add the lamb and cook, tossing to coat with the seasonings, until browned all over, 2 to 3 minutes.

3. Stir in the vegetable mixture and ½ cup of water. Cover, reduce the heat to low, and simmer until the lamb and vegetables are tender, 20 to 25 minutes.

4. In a medium saucepan, combine the broth and the remaining 2 tablespoons butter. Bring to a boil over high heat, then add the couscous, stirring until the grains are well moistened. Remove the pan from the heat, cover, and let the mixture stand for 5 minutes. Transfer the couscous to a serving platter.

5. Fold the tomatoes and parsley into the lamb mixture. Spoon the stew over the couscous on the platter.

BAKED EGGS
WITH PASTA AND PEPPERS

S E R V E S 4

3 RED BELL PEPPERS, CUT INTO 3 OR 4
FLAT PANELS, CORES AND SEEDS
DISCARDED
1 YELLOW BELL PEPPER, CUT INTO 3
OR 4 FLAT PANELS, CORES AND
SEEDS DISCARDED
1½ CUPS (LOOSELY PACKED) FRESH
BASIL OR PARSLEY LEAVES

4 GARLIC CLOVES, MINCED
½ CUP OLIVE OIL
¼ POUND FUSILLI PASTA
½ TEASPOON SALT
¼ TEASPOON BLACK PEPPER
8 EGGS
2 TABLESPOONS MINCED CHIVES
2 TABLESPOONS MINCED PARSLEY

1. Preheat the broiler. Place the pepper pieces, skin-side up, on a baking sheet and broil as close to the heat as possible for 10 minutes, or until evenly charred. Transfer the pepper pieces to a bowl and cover with a plate to steam the peppers. Set aside. Turn the oven to 350°.

2. Meanwhile, in a food processor, finely mince the basil and half of the garlic. With the machine running, add ¼ cup of the oil in a slow, steady stream, and process until a thick paste forms. Set aside.

3. In a large pot of boiling water, cook the pasta until al dente according to package directions. Drain, rinse the pasta under cold water, and drain well.

4. Peel the peppers and cut them lengthwise into ½-inch-wide strips.

5. In a medium bowl, combine the remaining ¼ cup oil with the remaining garlic, the salt, and black pepper, and stir to blend. Add the roasted pepper strips and toss gently.

6. Transfer the pasta to a large ovenproof skillet. Add the basil paste and toss to combine. Arrange the pepper strips over the pasta. Carefully break the eggs in a circle over the peppers. Sprinkle with the chives and parsley, cover, and bake for 20 to 25 minutes, or until the eggs are just set.

7. Serve from the skillet in wedges.

BELL PEPPERS STUFFED
WITH CORN, BEANS, AND RICE

SERVES 4

◇ LOW-FAT

1½ CUPS CHICKEN BROTH, PREFERABLY
   REDUCED-SODIUM

2 MEDIUM PLUM TOMATOES, COARSELY
   CHOPPED

1 SMALL ONION, COARSELY CHOPPED

¼ CUP MINCED FRESH BASIL, OR
   1 TEASPOON DRIED

3 GARLIC CLOVES, MINCED

2 TABLESPOONS FRESH LEMON JUICE

3 TEASPOONS GRATED LEMON ZEST

1 TEASPOON OREGANO

¼ TEASPOON BLACK PEPPER

½ CUP FROZEN CORN KERNELS

¾ CUP RICE

4 LARGE RED OR GREEN BELL PEPPERS

1 CUP CANNED BLACK BEANS, RINSED
   AND DRAINED

3 TABLESPOONS GRATED PARMESAN
   CHEESE

1. In a medium saucepan, bring the broth to a boil over medium-high heat. Add the tomatoes, onion, basil, garlic, lemon juice, lemon zest, oregano, black pepper, corn, and rice, and return to a boil. Reduce the heat to low, cover, and simmer until the rice is tender and the liquid is absorbed, about 20 minutes.

2. Preheat the oven to 350°. Line a shallow 9-inch square baking dish with foil.

3. Meanwhile, cut a thin slice from the top of each bell pepper; remove and discard the seeds. Stand the peppers upright in the prepared baking dish.

4. Stir the black beans into the cooked rice. Dividing evenly, stuff the peppers with the rice mixture. Top with the Parmesan cheese. Bake for 15 minutes, or until the cheese is almost golden.

KITCHEN NOTE: *For the most attractive meal, pick an assortment of peppers—red, green, yellow, or even orange and purple. Although the stuffed peppers are intended as a main dish, they can also serve as a substantial side dish with a simple entrée such as baked or grilled chicken or fish.*

Noodle-Stuffed Butternut Squash

SERVES 4

◇ LOW-FAT

2 MEDIUM BUTTERNUT SQUASH (ABOUT
2½ POUNDS EACH)
¼ POUND EGG NOODLES
1½ TEASPOONS OLIVE OIL
1 TABLESPOON UNSALTED BUTTER
1 MEDIUM ONION, COARSELY CHOPPED
2 GARLIC CLOVES, MINCED
1 MEDIUM RED OR GREEN BELL PEPPER,
COARSELY CHOPPED

¾ TEASPOON BASIL
¼ TEASPOON SALT
¼ TEASPOON BLACK PEPPER
¼ POUND HAM, PREFERABLY SMOKED,
CUT INTO ½-INCH CUBES
½ CUP SHREDDED SWISS CHEESE

1. Preheat the oven to 400°. Line a baking sheet with foil.

2. Halve the butternut squash lengthwise and remove the seeds and strings. Place the squash halves cut-side down on the prepared baking sheet and bake for 30 minutes, or until tender. When cool enough to handle, scoop out the flesh, leaving a scant ½-inch-thick shell. Coarsely chop the squash flesh.

3. Meanwhile, in a large pot of boiling water, cook the noodles until al dente according to package directions.

4. In a large skillet, warm the oil with the butter over medium-high heat until the butter is melted. Add the onion and garlic, and stir-fry until the onion begins to brown, about 5 minutes. Add the bell pepper, basil, salt, and black pepper, and cook until the bell pepper begins to soften, about 3 minutes. Remove the skillet from the heat.

5. Preheat the broiler. Drain the noodles and stir them into the skillet along with the ham, half of the cheese, and the chopped squash. Spoon the noodle stuffing into the squash shells and sprinkle with the remaining cheese.

6. Broil the stuffed squash 4 inches from the heat for 5 minutes, or until the cheese is bubbling and golden.

İtalian Vegetable Enchiladas

S E R V E S   4

◆ E X T R A - Q U I C K   ◇ L O W - F A T

1 TABLESPOON VEGETABLE OIL

1 GARLIC CLOVE, COARSELY CHOPPED

1 SMALL ONION, COARSELY CHOPPED

1 MEDIUM GREEN BELL PEPPER,
   COARSELY CHOPPED

½ POUND MUSHROOMS, COARSELY
   CHOPPED

1 MEDIUM TOMATO, COARSELY
   CHOPPED

ONE 8-OUNCE CAN NO-SALT-ADDED
   TOMATO SAUCE

½ TEASPOON BASIL

½ TEASPOON OREGANO

½ TEASPOON BLACK PEPPER

1 CUP LOW-FAT COTTAGE CHEESE

8 FLOUR TORTILLAS (7-INCH
   DIAMETER)

3 TABLESPOONS SHREDDED PART-SKIM
   MOZZARELLA CHEESE

1. In a large nonstick skillet, warm the oil over medium-high heat. Add the garlic, onion, bell pepper, mushrooms, and tomato, and cook, stirring occasionally, until the onion is slightly softened, about 3 minutes. Let cool slightly.

2. Meanwhile, in a medium bowl, combine the tomato sauce, ¼ teaspoon each of the basil, oregano, and black pepper.

3. In another bowl, combine the cottage cheese with the remaining ¼ teaspoon each basil, oregano, and black pepper.

4. Preheat the oven to 450°. Place the tortillas on the work surface and spread each evenly with 2 teaspoons of the tomato sauce. Spread 2 tablespoons of the cottage cheese in a strip along the bottom third of each tortilla.

5. Dividing evenly, spread the sautéed vegetable mixture over the cottage cheese. Starting at the filled end, roll the tortillas up. Place the rolled tortillas in a single layer in a large baking dish. Top with the remaining tomato sauce and the mozzarella.

6. Bake for 10 minutes, or until the tortillas are heated through and the cheese is melted. If desired, run the enchiladas under the broiler to lightly brown them.

Pasta Florentine

SERVES 4

◆ EXTRA-QUICK

½ POUND WAGON WHEEL PASTA OR
OTHER BITE-SIZE PASTA

½ POUND PART-SKIM MOZZARELLA
CHEESE, CUT INTO ¼-INCH CUBES

¼ POUND PROVOLONE CHEESE, CUT
INTO ¼-INCH CUBES

1 CUP GRATED PARMESAN CHEESE

ONE 10-OUNCE PACKAGE FROZEN
CHOPPED SPINACH, THAWED AND
SQUEEZED DRY

1 TEASPOON OREGANO

½ TEASPOON SALT

¼ TEASPOON NUTMEG

¼ TEASPOON BLACK PEPPER

¾ CUP MILK

½ CUP GRATED ROMANO CHEESE

1 TABLESPOON CHOPPED PARSLEY

1. In a large pot of boiling water, cook the pasta until al dente according to package directions.

2. Preheat the oven to 450°. Grease a shallow 2-quart casserole.

3. Drain the pasta well, then return it to the cooking pot. Add the mozzarella, Provolone, Parmesan, spinach, oregano, salt, nutmeg, and pepper, and toss to combine well.

4. Transfer the pasta mixture to the prepared casserole. Pour in the milk and sprinkle with the Romano and parsley. Bake for 10 minutes, or until the filling is bubbling and the top is golden.

5. Serve the pasta hot.

Variation: *Though the word "Florentine" usually denotes a dish made with spinach, you could take the liberty of substituting another green vegetable. Use 1½ to 2 cups of cooked, drained, chopped broccoli, Swiss chard, or kale.*

Stuffed Manicotti with Tomato Sauce

SERVES 6

2 TABLESPOONS OLIVE OIL

1 TABLESPOON UNSALTED BUTTER

5 GARLIC CLOVES, MINCED

2 MEDIUM ONIONS, CHOPPED

½ POUND CABBAGE, SHREDDED

1 MEDIUM CARROT, SHREDDED

1 UNPEELED GREEN APPLE, SHREDDED

1½ TEASPOONS OREGANO

1 CUP PART-SKIM RICOTTA CHEESE

1 EGG

1 CUP SHREDDED SWISS CHEESE

¾ TEASPOON SALT

¼ TEASPOON BLACK PEPPER

12 MANICOTTI OR OTHER LARGE PASTA
  TUBES

12 CANNED NO-SALT-ADDED WHOLE
  TOMATOES, DRAINED AND CHOPPED

2 TABLESPOONS TOMATO PASTE

2 TABLESPOONS CIDER VINEGAR

2 TEASPOONS BROWN SUGAR

¾ TEASPOON FENNEL SEEDS

¼ CUP RAISINS

1. In a large skillet, warm 1 tablespoon of the oil with the butter over medium-high heat until the butter is melted. Add half the garlic, half the onions, the cabbage, carrot, apple, and oregano, and cook, stirring, until the mixture begins to soften, about 4 minutes.

2. In a large bowl, combine the ricotta, egg, ½ cup of the Swiss cheese, ½ teaspoon of salt, and the pepper. Stir in the cooked vegetables.

3. Preheat the oven to 425°. Lightly oil a 13 x 9-inch baking dish.

4. In a large pot of boiling water, cook the pasta until al dente according to package directions. Drain, then rinse under cold water.

5. In a medium skillet, warm the remaining 1 tablespoon oil over medium-high heat. Add the remaining garlic and onions, and stir-fry until the mixture is golden, 3 to 4 minutes. Add the tomatoes, tomato paste, vinegar, brown sugar, fennel seeds, remaining ¼ teaspoon salt, and the raisins. Cover and simmer while you stuff the manicotti.

6. Fill each manicotti tube with about ⅓ cup of the cheese-vegetable filling. Place the filled manicotti in the baking dish. Spoon the sauce over the pasta, sprinkle the remaining ½ cup Swiss cheese on top, and bake for 20 minutes, or until heated through.

Baked Mushroom Manicotti with Three Cheeses

SERVES 4

8 MANICOTTI OR OTHER LARGE PASTA
   TUBES
1 TABLESPOON OLIVE OIL
2 GARLIC CLOVES, MINCED
1 MEDIUM ONION, FINELY CHOPPED
½ POUND MUSHROOMS, FINELY
   CHOPPED
1½ CUPS TOMATO PURÉE
2 TABLESPOONS TOMATO PASTE

1½ TEASPOONS OREGANO
1 BAY LEAF
ONE 15-OUNCE CONTAINER PART-SKIM
   RICOTTA CHEESE
½ CUP GRATED PARMESAN CHEESE
½ TEASPOON SALT
¼ TEASPOON BLACK PEPPER
⅔ CUP SHREDDED PART-SKIM
   MOZZARELLA CHEESE

1. In a large pot of boiling water, cook the pasta until almost al dente (it cooks more in the oven), about 9 minutes. Drain the pasta, rinse it under cold water to cool it off slightly, and drain again.

2. Meanwhile, in a medium skillet, warm the oil over medium-high heat. Add the garlic, onion, and mushrooms, and stir-fry until the onion is wilted and the mushrooms release some of their moisture, 2 to 3 minutes.

3. Remove half of the onion-mushroom mixture to a large bowl. To the vegetables remaining in the skillet, add the tomato purée, tomato paste, ½ teaspoon of the oregano, and the bay leaf. Bring the mixture to a boil over medium heat. Reduce the heat to medium-low and simmer, uncovered, while you stuff the pasta.

4. Preheat the oven to 375°.

5. To the onion-mushroom mixture in the bowl, add the ricotta, Parmesan, remaining 1 teaspoon oregano, the salt, and pepper. Stuff each manicotti with ¼ cup of the mixture.

6. Remove the tomato sauce from the heat. Remove and discard the bay leaf. Spread about ½ cup of the sauce in an 11 x 7-inch baking dish. Arrange the stuffed manicotti on top, cover the pasta with the remaining sauce, and sprinkle the mozzarella on top.

7. Bake for 25 minutes, or until the manicotti are heated through.

Pasta and Chicken Gratin

SERVES 6

♦ EXTRA-QUICK

2 CUPS CHICKEN BROTH, PREFERABLY
  REDUCED-SODIUM
3 GARLIC CLOVES, MINCED
1 CUP ORZO OR OTHER SMALL PASTA
  SHAPE
3 TABLESPOONS OLIVE OIL
1 LARGE ONION, THINLY SLICED
2 MEDIUM ZUCCHINI, DICED
1½ TEASPOONS OREGANO
¼ TEASPOON SALT
½ TEASPOON BLACK PEPPER

1 TABLESPOON FINE UNSEASONED DRY
  BREAD CRUMBS
1 TABLESPOON GRATED PARMESAN
  CHEESE
½ POUND SKINLESS, BONELESS
  CHICKEN BREASTS, CUT ACROSS THE
  GRAIN INTO ¼-INCH-WIDE SLICES
¼ POUND SWISS CHEESE, SHREDDED
½ CUP SHREDDED PART-SKIM
  MOZZARELLA CHEESE
¼ CUP CHOPPED PARSLEY (OPTIONAL)

1. In a medium saucepan, bring the broth and half the garlic to a boil over high heat. Add the orzo; reduce the heat to low, cover, and simmer until al dente according to package directions. Remove from the heat; do not drain.

2. Meanwhile, in a large broilerproof skillet, warm 1 tablespoon of the oil over medium-high heat. Add the remaining garlic and the onion, and stir-fry until the onion begins to brown, about 5 minutes.

3. Add the zucchini, oregano, salt, and pepper, and stir-fry until the zucchini begins to soften, about 3 minutes. Transfer to a plate and cover loosely with foil to keep warm.

4. Preheat the broiler. In a small bowl, combine the bread crumbs and Parmesan.

5. Add 1 tablespoon of the oil to the skillet. Add the chicken and stir-fry until the chicken is just cooked through, about 3 minutes. Reduce the heat to medium.

6. Return the vegetables to the skillet. Add the cooked orzo and broth mixture, the Swiss cheese, mozzarella, and parsley (if using), and stir to combine. Sprinkle the bread crumb mixture over the pasta mixture and drizzle with the remaining 1 tablespoon oil. Broil 4 inches from the heat until the top is golden, 3 to 5 minutes. Serve directly from the skillet.

DILLED CHICKEN BAKE
WITH POTATOES AND CARROTS

SERVES 4

2½ POUNDS CHICKEN PARTS

1 MEDIUM ONION, CUT INTO ½-INCH
WEDGES

2 GARLIC CLOVES, MINCED

1½ POUNDS ALL-PURPOSE POTATOES,
PEELED AND CUT INTO CHUNKS

2 LARGE CARROTS, CUT INTO CHUNKS

3 TABLESPOONS CHOPPED FRESH DILL,
OR 1 TABLESPOON DRIED

1 TEASPOON SALT

½ TEASPOON BLACK PEPPER

2 TABLESPOONS FLOUR

⅔ CUP CHICKEN BROTH, PREFERABLY
REDUCED-SODIUM

1. Preheat the oven to 375°.

2. In a large flameproof casserole or Dutch oven, cook the chicken skin-side down over medium heat for 5 minutes to render some of its fat. Increase the heat to medium-high and continue cooking until browned on all sides, about 5 minutes per side. Remove the chicken to a plate and cover loosely with foil to keep warm.

3. Warm the pan drippings in the casserole over medium-high heat. Add the onion and garlic, and cook until golden, about 3 minutes. Add the potatoes and carrots, and cook, stirring, until the vegetables are well coated with the pan drippings, about 1 minute.

4. Return the chicken (and any juices that have collected on the plate) to the casserole and remove from the heat. Stir in 1 tablespoon of the dill (fresh or dried), the salt, and pepper. Cover and bake for 10 minutes.

5. Remove the casserole from the oven, stir to redistribute the chicken and vegetables, re-cover and bake for another 15 minutes, or until the the chicken is cooked through.

6. With a slotted spoon, transfer the ingredients to a platter. Add the flour to the casserole and cook over medium-high heat, stirring, until the flour is no longer visible, about 30 seconds. Stir in the chicken broth and cook, stirring, until the gravy is slightly thickened, 1 to 2 minutes.

7. Serve the chicken and vegetables sprinkled with the remaining fresh dill (if using) and pass the gravy separately.

Chicken with Vegetables in Apple-Cider Sauce

SERVES 4

6 CUPS UNSWEETENED APPLE CIDER

3 MEDIUM LEEKS, CUT INTO ¼-INCH SLICES

16 RED CABBAGE LEAVES

2 GARLIC CLOVES, PEELED

4 SKINLESS, BONELESS CHICKEN BREAST HALVES (ABOUT 1½ POUNDS TOTAL)

6 MEDIUM CARROTS, CUT INTO MATCHSTICKS

3 MEDIUM ZUCCHINI, CUT INTO ½-INCH SLICES

1½ TABLESPOONS RED WINE VINEGAR

1½ TABLESPOONS DIJON MUSTARD

1. In a saucepan large enough to hold a steamer insert or colander, bring the cider to a boil over high heat. Add the leeks, cabbage leaves, and whole garlic. Reduce the heat to low and simmer for 5 minutes.

2. Add the chicken and return the liquid to a boil over medium-high heat. Cover, reduce the heat to low, and simmer for 10 minutes.

3. Place a steamer insert or a colander in the pan. Add the carrots to the steamer insert, cover, and steam for 3 minutes. Add the zucchini to the steamer insert, cover, and steam until the carrots and zucchini are crisp-tender, about 3 minutes.

4. Remove the steamer insert and divide the zucchini and carrots among 4 dinner plates. With a slotted spoon, remove the remaining vegetables and chicken from the poaching liquid and add to the dinner plates. Cover loosely with foil to keep warm.

5. Discard the garlic and bring the poaching liquid to a boil. Cook, uncovered, until the liquid is reduced to about 2 cups, 6 to 10 minutes. Whisk in the vinegar and mustard, and cook until the sauce is syrupy, 5 to 7 minutes.

6. Spoon the cider sauce over the chicken and vegetables, and serve hot.

CHICKEN WITH POTATOES, PEPPERS, AND ZUCCHINI

SERVES 4

3 GARLIC CLOVES, MINCED

3 TABLESPOONS OLIVE OIL

2 TEASPOONS OREGANO

1½ TEASPOONS THYME

½ TEASPOON RED PEPPER FLAKES

1 TEASPOON SALT

¾ TEASPOON BLACK PEPPER

1 POUND SMALL UNPEELED RED POTATOES, THINLY SLICED

2 MEDIUM ONIONS, THINLY SLICED

1 MEDIUM YELLOW OR RED BELL PEPPER, CUT INTO THIN STRIPS

1 MEDIUM GREEN BELL PEPPER, CUT INTO THIN STRIPS

4 SMALL PLUM TOMATOES, THINLY SLICED

1 MEDIUM ZUCCHINI, THINLY SLICED

1 BAY LEAF

1 TEASPOON UNSALTED BUTTER

4 BONE-IN CHICKEN BREAST HALVES (ABOUT 2 POUNDS TOTAL)

¼ CUP DRY WHITE WINE OR CHICKEN BROTH

2 TEASPOONS BASIL

1. Preheat the oven to 425°. In a small bowl, combine the garlic, 2 tablespoons of the oil, 1½ teaspoons of the oregano, the thyme, red pepper flakes, and ½ teaspoon each of the salt and black pepper, and stir to blend.

2. In a large casserole or Dutch oven, combine the potatoes and onions, drizzle 1 tablespoon of the herbed oil over them, and toss to coat. Bake the casserole for 10 minutes.

3. Add the bell peppers, tomatoes, and zucchini to the casserole, and drizzle the remaining herbed oil over them. Add the bay leaf, return the casserole to the oven, and continue to bake while you brown the chicken.

4. In a large skillet, warm the remaining 1 tablespoon oil with the butter over medium-high heat. Add the chicken, skin-side down, and cook until browned, about 5 minutes per side. Add the chicken to the casserole, cover, and return to the oven.

5. In the same skillet, pour in the wine. Add the basil, and the remaining ½ teaspoon oregano, ½ teaspoon salt, and ¼ teaspoon black pepper. Bring to a boil, stirring to incorporate any browned bits in the pan. Pour this mixture over the chicken, re-cover, and bake for 20 to 25 minutes, or until the chicken is tender. Remove and discard the bay leaf.

ROASTED SALMON AND VEGETABLES

SERVES 4

¼ CUP OLIVE OIL

¼ CUP CHOPPED PARSLEY (OPTIONAL)

2 GARLIC CLOVES, MINCED

¾ TEASPOON SALT

¼ TEASPOON BLACK PEPPER

8 SMALL UNPEELED RED POTATOES,
QUARTERED

2 LARGE CARROTS, CUT ON THE
DIAGONAL INTO ½-INCH SLICES

3 SCALLIONS, CUT INTO 2-INCH PIECES

½ POUND SMALL MUSHROOMS

1 POUND SALMON FILLET, CUT INTO
1½-INCH CUBES

1. Preheat the oven to 450°.

2. In a medium bowl, combine the oil, parsley (if using), garlic, salt, and pepper, and mix to blend.

3. Scatter the potatoes, carrots, scallions, and mushrooms in a shallow 1½-quart baking dish. Drizzle 2 tablespoons of the garlic oil over them and toss gently to coat.

4. Place the dish in the oven and roast for 30 minutes, or until the potatoes are almost done and beginning to brown; stir the vegetables once or twice to ensure even cooking.

5. Add the salmon to the bowl of remaining garlic oil and toss gently to coat.

6. Lower the oven temperature to 375°. Stir the vegetables in the baking dish, scatter the salmon on top, and roast for 10 minutes, or until the vegetables are tender and the fish just flakes when tested with a fork.

STUFFED ZUCCHINI BOATS

SERVES 4

♦ EXTRA-QUICK

⅔ CUP BEEF BROTH

2 GARLIC CLOVES, MINCED

¾ TEASPOON BASIL

¼ TEASPOON BLACK PEPPER

4 MEDIUM ZUCCHINI, HALVED
  LENGTHWISE

½ POUND LEAN GROUND BEEF

2 TEASPOONS CORNSTARCH

1 LARGE OR 2 SMALL PLUM TOMATOES,
  COARSELY CHOPPED

⅓ CUP SHREDDED PART-SKIM
  MOZZARELLA

1. In a large skillet, bring the broth, garlic, basil, and pepper to a boil over medium-high heat. Add the zucchini halves, reduce the heat to low, cover, and simmer until they are barely tender, about 5 minutes.

2. Transfer the zucchini to a plate and set aside to cool slightly. Measure out and remove ¼ cup of the broth, leaving the remainder in the skillet.

3. Increase the heat under the skillet to medium. Crumble in the ground beef and cook, stirring occasionally to break it up, until the meat is no longer pink, about 5 minutes.

4. Meanwhile, carefully scoop out the zucchini flesh, leaving a ¼-inch-thick shell. Coarsely chop the flesh.

5. Preheat the broiler. Line a baking sheet with foil.

6. In a small bowl, combine the reserved ¼ cup of broth with the cornstarch, and stir to combine. Bring the beef mixture to a boil over medium-high heat. Add the chopped zucchini and the cornstarch mixture, and cook, stirring, until the liquid has thickened, about 1 minute. Remove the skillet from the heat and stir in the tomatoes.

7. Place the zucchini halves on the prepared baking sheet. Dividing evenly, mound the beef mixture into the hollowed-out zucchini and sprinkle with the mozzarella. Broil 4 inches from the heat for 2 to 3 minutes, or until the cheese is melted and bubbling.

Meat-and-Potatoes Loaf

SERVES 6

5 MEDIUM CARROTS, CUT INTO 1-INCH
   LENGTHS
1 LARGE YELLOW OR RED BELL PEPPER,
   CUT INTO LARGE PIECES
5 MEDIUM SCALLIONS, MINCED
½ POUND LEAN GROUND BEEF
½ POUND GROUND VEAL
⅔ CUP BOTTLED BARBECUE SAUCE
¾ CUP FINE UNSEASONED DRY BREAD
   CRUMBS
2 TABLESPOONS TOMATO PASTE

3 TABLESPOONS BUTTER, MELTED
1 TABLESPOON BROWN SUGAR
1 TEASPOON BASIL
¾ TEASPOON SALT
1 TEASPOON BLACK PEPPER
1¼ POUNDS UNPEELED RED POTATOES,
   SHREDDED
1 TABLESPOON FLOUR
1 EGG
⅓ CUP GRATED PARMESAN CHEESE

1. Preheat the oven to 425°. Butter a shallow 2-quart baking dish.

2. In a medium saucepan, bring 2 inches of water to a boil. Add the carrots and bell pepper, and return to a boil. Reduce the heat to low, cover, and simmer until the carrots are tender, about 7 minutes.

3. Meanwhile, in a large bowl, combine the scallions, beef, veal, barbecue sauce, and ½ cup of the bread crumbs; mix well. Set aside.

4. Drain the carrots and bell pepper and place them in a food processor. Add the tomato paste, 1 tablespoon of the melted butter, the brown sugar, basil, ½ teaspoon of the salt, ¼ teaspoon of the black pepper, and the remaining ¼ cup bread crumbs. Process to just combine. Cool slightly.

5. In a medium bowl, toss the potatoes with the flour. In a small bowl, beat the egg with the remaining 2 tablespoons melted butter, ¼ teaspoon salt, and ¾ teaspoon black pepper. Add the egg mixture to the potatoes and toss to combine.

6. Spread half of the potatoes in the prepared baking dish. Spread the carrot mixture on top. Spread the meat mixture on top of the carrot layer. Spread the remaining potatoes on top.

7. Sprinkle the Parmesan cheese on top and bake for 1 hour, or until the meat is cooked through and the topping is golden brown.

Zucchini-Beef Moussaka

SERVES 4

1 LARGE FRESH TOMATO OR 2 CANNED
   TOMATOES, COARSELY CHOPPED
1 MEDIUM ONION, COARSELY CHOPPED
3 GARLIC CLOVES, MINCED
1 POUND LEAN GROUND BEEF
3 TABLESPOONS TOMATO PASTE
1 TEASPOON CINNAMON
1 TEASPOON OREGANO

½ TEASPOON SALT
¼ TEASPOON BLACK PEPPER
2 TABLESPOONS CORNSTARCH
1 MEDIUM ZUCCHINI, THINLY SLICED
¾ CUP GRATED PARMESAN CHEESE
1 EGG
⅔ CUP REDUCED-FAT SOUR CREAM
2 TABLESPOONS FLOUR

1. Preheat the oven to 375°.

2. In a medium saucepan, combine the tomato, onion, garlic, ground beef, tomato paste, cinnamon, oregano, salt, and pepper. Bring the mixture to a boil over medium heat, stirring and breaking up the meat with a spoon. Reduce the heat to low, cover, and simmer for 10 minutes.

3. In a plastic or paper bag, shake the cornstarch and zucchini together to coat.

4. In a shallow 1½-quart baking dish, layer half the meat-tomato sauce, half the zucchini, and ¼ cup of the Parmesan. Top with the re-

maining meat-tomato sauce and zucchini. Sprinkle with ¼ cup of the Parmesan.

5. In a small bowl, lightly beat the egg. Blend in the sour cream, flour, and remaining ¼ cup Parmesan.

6. Spoon the sour cream mixture evenly over the top of the casserole and bake for 30 minutes, or until the top is light golden and the moussaka is heated through.

SWEET AFTERTHOUGHT: *You'd do well to follow this filling Greek specialty with a light Mediterranean-style dessert: Simply offer a platter of figs and unshelled almonds. Though fresh figs are delicious, they are often hard to find. Instead you can present a variety of dried figs, including the popular Calimyrnas, plump Mission figs, and the chewy Greek figs sold strung on a length of vine.*

VEGETABLE-RICE CASSEROLE WITH HAM

SERVES 6

1 CUP CHICKEN BROTH, PREFERABLY
   REDUCED-SODIUM
1 CUP MILK
¾ CUP RICE
ONE 10-OUNCE PACKAGE FROZEN
   CORN KERNELS
ONE 10-OUNCE PACKAGE FROZEN PEAS
2 TABLESPOONS FLOUR
1 TEASPOON OREGANO

¼ TEASPOON BLACK PEPPER
8 SCALLIONS, COARSELY CHOPPED
½ POUND HAM, CUT INTO ½-INCH
   CUBES
1 CUP SHREDDED CHEDDAR CHEESE
¼ CUP CHOPPED PARSLEY (OPTIONAL)
ONE 3-OUNCE PACKAGE CREAM
   CHEESE, AT ROOM TEMPERATURE

1. Preheat the oven to 425°. Butter a 13 x 9-inch baking dish.

2. In a medium saucepan, bring the broth and milk to a boil over medium heat. Add the rice and cook for 10 minutes.

3. Meanwhile, in a large bowl, combine the corn and peas, and break them up to separate. Stir in the flour, oregano, and pepper.

4. Add the scallions and ham to the vegetables in the bowl. Add the Cheddar and parsley (if using), and stir to blend.

5. In a small bowl, beat the cream cheese to soften it. Measure out about ⅓ cup of the hot milk-broth mixture from the saucepan and stir it into the cream cheese until smooth. Stir the softened cream cheese into the vegetable-ham mixture. Then stir in the remaining rice with its liquid.

6. Transfer the mixture to the prepared baking dish and cover tightly with foil. Bake for 35 to 40 minutes, or until the rice is tender; stir several times for even cooking.

HAM AND CHEESE LASAGNA WITH SPINACH

SERVES 8

½ POUND LASAGNA NOODLES

ONE 15-OUNCE CONTAINER PART-SKIM RICOTTA CHEESE

1 POUND LOW-FAT COTTAGE CHEESE

1 CUP GRATED PARMESAN CHEESE

¼ CUP FLOUR

1 TEASPOON NUTMEG

½ TEASPOON SALT

½ TEASPOON BLACK PEPPER

3 EGGS

ONE 10-OUNCE PACKAGE FROZEN SPINACH, THAWED AND SQUEEZED DRY

¼ POUND SLICED SWISS CHEESE, CUT INTO THIN STRIPS

¼ POUND SLICED HAM, CUT INTO THIN STRIPS

1. In a large pot of boiling water, cook the noodles until al dente according to package directions. Drain the noodles, rinse under cold running water, and drain again.

2. Meanwhile, in a large bowl, combine the ricotta, cottage cheese, Parmesan, flour, nutmeg, salt, and pepper. Lightly beat the eggs and then stir them into the cheese mixture.

3. Finely chop the spinach and stir it into the cheese mixture.

4. Preheat the oven to 375°. Lightly oil a 13 x 9-inch baking pan.

5. Layer the lasagna in the following manner: one-third of the noodles, one-third of the Swiss cheese strips, one-third of the ham strips, and one-third of the spinach-cheese mixture. Repeat for two more layers.

6. Bake the lasagna for 45 minutes, or until the top is golden brown.

LAYERED HAM AND POTATO CASSEROLE

SERVES 4

1 POUND UNPEELED RED POTATOES,
  CUT INTO ¼-INCH SLICES

1 MEDIUM RED ONION, COARSELY
  CHOPPED

1 MEDIUM STALK BROCCOLI, COARSELY
  CHOPPED

½ POUND UNSLICED LEAN HAM, CUT
  INTO ½-INCH CUBES

⅔ CUP FLOUR

2 CUPS MILK

2 TABLESPOONS DIJON MUSTARD

1 TEASPOON SALT

½ TEASPOON BLACK PEPPER

2 TABLESPOONS UNSALTED BUTTER

1. Preheat the oven to 350°. Lightly butter a shallow 1½-quart baking dish.

2. In a large bowl, combine the potatoes, onion, broccoli, ham, and flour. Toss to distribute the ingredients evenly. Spread the mixture in the prepared baking dish.

3. In a small bowl, beat the milk, mustard, salt, and pepper together. Pour the milk mixture over the vegetables and ham in the baking dish. Dot with the butter.

4. Cover the dish with foil and bake for 30 minutes. Uncover and bake for 45 minutes, or until the top is browned and the potatoes are tender.

Variation: *This is a dish to keep in mind when you have leftover turkey on hand. Add about 1 cup of diced, cooked turkey in place of the ham. Increase the mustard by 1 or 2 teaspoons, and sprinkle the top of the casserole with 2 tablespoons of grated Parmesan before putting it in the oven.*

ALSATIAN SAUSAGE AND CABBAGE CASSEROLE

SERVES 6

½ POUND SAUERKRAUT

1 POUND SMALL UNPEELED RED
POTATOES, THINLY SLICED

1 TEASPOON OLIVE OIL

4 SLICES OF BACON

2 LARGE ONIONS, COARSELY CHOPPED

3 GARLIC CLOVES, MINCED

½ POUND CABBAGE, FINELY SHREDDED

¼ CUP CHOPPED PARSLEY

¾ TEASPOON CUMIN

½ TEASPOON BLACK PEPPER

1 POUND KIELBASA OR OTHER FULLY
COOKED GARLIC SAUSAGE, CUT INTO
¾-INCH CHUNKS

½ POUND SKINLESS, BONELESS
CHICKEN BREAST, CUT INTO ¾-INCH
CHUNKS

1 BAY LEAF

1 CUP DRY WHITE WINE OR CHICKEN
BROTH

1. Preheat the oven to 400°. Soak the sauer-kraut in a bowl of cold water while you prepare the remaining ingredients.

2. Layer the potatoes in a shallow 2-quart casserole. Sprinkle the oil on top and toss the potatoes to coat. Bake, uncovered, for 20 minutes (potatoes will not be fully cooked).

3. Meanwhile, in a large nonstick skillet, cook the bacon over medium heat until crisp, about 10 minutes. Drain the bacon on paper towels; crumble and set aside. Pour off all but 2 tablespoons of the fat in the skillet.

4. Add the onions and garlic to the fat in the skillet and cook over medium-high heat until softened, 3 to 4 minutes. Add the cabbage and

cook, stirring, until slightly wilted, about 3 minutes. Remove the skillet from the heat.

5. Drain the sauerkraut, rinse under cold running water, and drain again. Squeeze the sauerkraut dry and add it to the skillet. Stir in the bacon, parsley, cumin, and pepper.

6. Remove the potatoes from the oven; leave the oven on. Stir the potatoes gently, then add half of the cabbage mixture, all the kielbasa and chicken, and the bay leaf. Pour in the wine. Top with the remaining cabbage mixture.

7. Cover and bake for 30 minutes, or until the potatoes and chicken are tender. Remove and discard the bay leaf before serving.

Italian-Style Stuffed Peppers

SERVES 4

1 POUND SWEET ITALIAN SAUSAGES, CASINGS REMOVED

½ CUP GRATED PARMESAN CHEESE

½ CUP PLUS 2 TABLESPOONS FRESH BREAD CRUMBS

⅓ CUP MINCED ONION

⅓ CUP FINELY CHOPPED PARSLEY

3 TABLESPOONS PINE NUTS

½ TEASPOON OREGANO

PINCH OF BLACK PEPPER

4 MEDIUM GREEN BELL PEPPERS

2 TABLESPOONS OLIVE OIL

1. Preheat the oven to 350°.

2. Crumble the sausage into a large bowl. Add ¼ cup of the Parmesan, ½ cup of the bread crumbs, the onion, parsley, pine nuts, oregano, and black pepper, and stir to mix.

3. Cut a ½-inch-thick slice from the top of each pepper; remove and discard the core and seeds. Mince the tops and add them to the sausage mixture.

4. Place the peppers in a 9-inch square baking dish. Divide the sausage stuffing among the peppers, mounding slightly if necessary, and drizzle with the oil. Bake the peppers for 35 minutes.

5. Meanwhile, in a small bowl, combine the remaining ¼ cup Parmesan and 2 tablespoons bread crumbs.

6. Increase the oven temperature to 375°, sprinkle the peppers with the Parmesan mixture, and bake for 10 minutes, or until the stuffing is cooked through and the topping is golden.

KITCHEN NOTE: *Pine nuts, also called pignoli, are the seeds of one of several varieties of pine tree that grow in the Mediterranean and the American Southwest. Pine nuts are sold in small jars in the Italian foods section of most supermarkets. Because of their high fat content, it's best to store pine nuts in a tightly closed container in the freezer so they do not become rancid.*

SAUSAGE, LENTIL, AND MUSHROOM CASSEROLE

SERVES 4

2 TABLESPOONS OLIVE OIL

1 POUND FULLY COOKED SMOKED SAUSAGE, CUT INTO BITE-SIZE PIECES

2 MEDIUM ONIONS, COARSELY CHOPPED

3 GARLIC CLOVES, MINCED

1 TEASPOON THYME

1 BAY LEAF

3 CUPS REDUCED-SODIUM CHICKEN BROTH

1¼ CUPS LENTILS, RINSED AND PICKED OVER

½ TEASPOON SALT

¼ TEASPOON BLACK PEPPER

2 TABLESPOONS UNSALTED BUTTER

¾ POUND MUSHROOMS, QUARTERED

¼ CUP CHOPPED PARSLEY

2 TABLESPOONS GRATED PARMESAN CHEESE

2 TABLESPOONS FINE UNSEASONED DRY BREAD CRUMBS

1. In a large saucepan, warm 1 tablespoon of the oil over medium-high heat. Add the sausage and cook until browned, about 10 minutes. Transfer to a plate and set aside.

2. Add the onions, garlic, thyme, and bay leaf to the pan. Cover and cook, stirring occasionally, until softened, about 10 minutes.

3. Stir in the broth, lentils, salt, and black pepper. Return the sausage to the pan. Bring to a boil, reduce the heat to medium-low, and cook, uncovered, stirring occasionally, until the lentils are just tender, about 25 minutes.

4. Meanwhile, in a medium skillet, warm the butter over medium heat until melted. Add the mushrooms and cook, tossing and stirring, until tender, about 10 minutes. Set aside.

5. Preheat the oven to 400°. In a small bowl, combine the parsley, Parmesan, and bread crumbs.

6. Stir the mushrooms into the lentils. Remove and discard the bay leaf. Transfer the mixture to a shallow 1½-quart baking dish. Sprinkle the bread crumb mixture on top, drizzle with the remaining 1 tablespoon oil, and bake for 25 minutes, or until the lentils are bubbling and the top is crisp and brown.

7. Serve the casserole hot.

Hot Pepper Quiche

SERVES 6

1 TABLESPOON UNSALTED BUTTER

8 SCALLIONS, COARSELY CHOPPED

3 GARLIC CLOVES, MINCED

1 TABLESPOON OLIVE OIL

1 MEDIUM GREEN BELL PEPPER, THINLY SLICED

1 SMALL YELLOW SQUASH, THINLY SLICED

1 MEDIUM PLUM TOMATO, COARSELY CHOPPED

ONE 10-OUNCE PACKAGE FROZEN CORN KERNELS, THAWED

2 TABLESPOONS FLOUR

1 TABLESPOON CHILI POWDER

1 TABLESPOON CUMIN

½ TEASPOON SALT

PINCH OF CAYENNE PEPPER

4 EGGS

⅓ CUP MILK

¼ POUND SHREDDED PEPPER JACK CHEESE

ONE 9-INCH PIE SHELL, STORE-BOUGHT OR HOMEMADE

1. Preheat the oven to 375°. Line a baking sheet with foil.

2. In a large skillet, warm the butter over medium heat until melted. Add the scallions and garlic, and cook, stirring, until the scallions are softened, about 5 minutes.

3. Add the olive oil, bell pepper, and squash, and cook, stirring, until the vegetables are softened, about 4 minutes.

4. Add the tomato, corn, flour, chili powder, cumin, salt, and cayenne, and cook, stirring, until the flour is no longer visible, about 30 seconds. Remove from the heat.

5. In a medium bowl, beat the eggs with the milk. Add the sautéed vegetables and the shredded cheese, and stir to combine.

6. Spoon the vegetable-cheese filling into the pie shell. Place the pie shell on the baking sheet and bake for 50 minutes, or until the filling is set and the top is golden. Let cool for 10 minutes before slicing.

POLENTA PIZZA

SERVES 4

◇ LOW-FAT

½ TEASPOON SALT

3 CUPS CORNMEAL

1 TABLESPOON OLIVE OIL

1 MEDIUM RED ONION, FINELY SLICED

1 LARGE GARLIC CLOVE, CHOPPED

2 MEDIUM CARROTS, CHOPPED

4 CELERY RIBS, FINELY SLICED

3 MEDIUM TOMATOES, CHOPPED

6 TABLESPOONS TOMATO PASTE

1 TEASPOON BASIL

½ TEASPOON OREGANO

¼ TEASPOON BLACK PEPPER

PINCH OF CAYENNE PEPPER

¼ POUND PART-SKIM MOZZARELLA CHEESE, VERY THINLY SLICED

1 TABLESPOON GRATED PARMESAN CHEESE

1. Preheat the oven to 350°. Lightly oil a 13 x 9-inch baking pan.

2. In a large saucepan, combine 9 cups of water with the salt and bring to a boil over medium-high heat. Sprinkle in the cornmeal, stirring constantly with a wooden spoon. Reduce the heat to medium and cook the polenta, stirring constantly, until all the liquid has been absorbed and the polenta is quite stiff, 10 to 15 minutes.

3. Spoon the polenta into the prepared baking pan and spread it out to a uniform thickness. Cover the pan with foil and bake for 20 minutes.

4. Meanwhile, in a medium saucepan, warm the oil over medium heat. Add the onion and sauté until very tender, about 10 minutes. Add the garlic, carrots, celery, and tomatoes, and cook, stirring frequently, for 5 minutes.

5. In a cup, combine the tomato paste and ¾ cup of hot water, and stir to blend. Stir the tomato paste mixture into the vegetable mixture. Add the basil, oregano, black pepper, and cayenne. Cover, reduce the heat to low, and simmer the sauce for 15 minutes.

6. When the polenta is ready, spread the sauce over it. Cover the sauce with the mozzarella slices, then sprinkle with the Parmesan cheese. Return the polenta to the oven for 10 minutes, or until the cheese has melted. Serve the pizza hot.

Topsy-Turvy Pizza

SERVES 6

1 TABLESPOON OLIVE OIL

1 MEDIUM ONION, COARSELY CHOPPED

3 GARLIC CLOVES, COARSELY CHOPPED

¼ POUND MUSHROOMS, COARSELY
  CHOPPED

½ POUND SWEET ITALIAN SAUSAGE,
  CASINGS REMOVED

ONE 8-OUNCE CAN TOMATO SAUCE

½ CUP CHOPPED PITTED BLACK OLIVES
  (OPTIONAL)

1 TEASPOON BASIL

½ TEASPOON OREGANO

¼ TEASPOON BLACK PEPPER

1 CUP FLOUR

1 TEASPOON BAKING POWDER

3 TABLESPOONS UNSALTED BUTTER,
  CUT INTO SMALL CHUNKS

1½ CUPS SHREDDED PART-SKIM
  MOZZARELLA CHEESE

ABOUT ¼ CUP MILK

1. In a 9-inch ovenproof skillet, warm the oil over medium-high heat. Add the onion, garlic, and mushrooms, and cook, stirring, until the onion begins to brown, about 5 minutes.

2. Crumble the sausage into the skillet. Cook, breaking up the sausage with a spoon, until the meat loses its pinkness, about 5 minutes. Drain any excess fat from the pan.

3. Preheat the oven to 425°.

4. Add the tomato sauce, olives (if using), basil, oregano, and pepper to the pan. Bring the mixture to a boil. Reduce the heat to medium-low and simmer, uncovered, while you make the topping.

5. In a food processor, combine the flour and baking powder. With the machine running,

add the butter, a chunk at a time, and process until the mixture resembles cornmeal. Pulse in ½ cup of the mozzarella. With the machine running, add just enough milk so the mixture forms a soft dough.

6. Turn the dough out onto a lightly floured work surface and roll out to a circle 9 inches in diameter (and about ¼ inch thick).

7. Remove the skillet from the heat, then sprinkle the remaining 1 cup mozzarella over the tomato-sausage sauce. Lay the circle of dough on top. Place the skillet in the oven and bake for 20 minutes, or until the top is golden. Serve hot, directly from the skillet.

Rustic Pizza Pie

SERVES 8

1 PACKAGE RAPID-RISE YEAST

¾ CUP HOT (125° TO 130°) WATER

¼ CUP OLIVE OIL

½ TEASPOON SALT

ABOUT 3½ CUPS PLUS ⅓ CUP FLOUR

1 MEDIUM ONION, COARSELY CHOPPED

3 GARLIC CLOVES, MINCED

1 WHOLE EGG PLUS 1 EGG YOLK

2 CUPS PART-SKIM RICOTTA CHEESE

½ CUP PLUS 1 TABLESPOON GRATED
  PARMESAN CHEESE

¼ POUND SMOKED CHEESE, DICED

3 OUNCES CREAM CHEESE, AT ROOM
  TEMPERATURE

1 CUP CORN KERNELS

ONE 10-OUNCE PACKAGE FROZEN
  CHOPPED SPINACH, THAWED AND
  SQUEEZED DRY

1 TEASPOON BASIL

1 TEASPOON OREGANO

¼ TEASPOON BLACK PEPPER

1 TABLESPOON MILK

1. Preheat the oven to 425°. Lightly oil an 8-inch round cake pan.

2. In a food processor, dissolve the yeast in the hot water. With the processor running, add 3 tablespoons of the oil, the salt, and 3¼ cups of the flour, and process until it forms a ball. If the dough is sticky, add up to ¼ cup flour. If it is dry, add 2 to 3 tablespoons water.

3. Divide the dough into two balls, one twice as big the other. Roll the larger of the two into a 11-inch circle. Roll the smaller piece into a 9-inch circle. Cover the dough with a towel.

4. In a medium skillet, warm the remaining 1 tablespoon oil over medium-high heat. Add the onion and garlic, and sauté until the onion begins to brown, about 3 minutes.

5. In a medium bowl, beat the whole egg and egg yolk with the ricotta. Beat in the onion mixture, ½ cup of the Parmesan, the smoked cheese, and cream cheese. Stir in the remaining ⅓ cup flour, the corn, spinach, basil, oregano, and pepper.

6. Fit the larger circle of dough into the cake pan; trim to a ½-inch overhang. Spoon the filling into the pan, top with the small dough circle, and pinch the edges together to seal.

7. Brush the pizza with the milk and sprinkle with the remaining 1 tablespoon Parmesan. Cut two or three steam vents and bake for 20 minutes, or until the crust is golden. Let stand for about 20 minutes before serving.

GROUND TURKEY PIZZA

SERVES 8

1 TABLESPOON PLUS 1 TEASPOON OLIVE
  OIL
½ CUP FINELY CHOPPED ONION
1 LARGE GREEN OR RED BELL PEPPER,
  CUT INTO THIN STRIPS
1½ CUPS THINLY SLICED MUSHROOMS
ONE 35-OUNCE CAN NO-SALT-ADDED
  WHOLE TOMATOES
2 LARGE GARLIC CLOVES, MINCED
2 TABLESPOONS RED WINE VINEGAR
2 TEASPOONS SUGAR
1 TEASPOON BASIL
½ TEASPOON OREGANO

½ TEASPOON SALT
½ TEASPOON BLACK PEPPER
½ CUP FINE UNSEASONED DRY BREAD
  CRUMBS
1 SCALLION, CHOPPED
2 EGG WHITES, LIGHTLY BEATEN
4 DROPS OF HOT PEPPER SAUCE
2 TABLESPOONS DRY WHITE WINE
2 POUNDS GROUND TURKEY
¾ CUP SHREDDED PART-SKIM
  MOZZARELLA CHEESE
½ CUP SHREDDED SWISS CHEESE

1. In a medium saucepan, warm 1 tablespoon of the oil over medium-low heat. Add the onion and cook, stirring frequently, for 3 minutes. Add the bell pepper strips and mushrooms and cook for 2 minutes.

2. Add the tomatoes, garlic, vinegar, sugar, basil, oregano, and ¼ teaspoon each of the salt and black pepper. Bring to a boil, reduce the heat to low, and simmer the pizza sauce gently, stirring occasionally, for 40 minutes.

3. Preheat the oven to 400°. Oil a shallow 10- to 12-inch round baking dish.

4. In a large bowl, combine the bread crumbs, scallion, egg whites, hot pepper

sauce, remaining 1 teaspoon oil, and the remaining ¼ teaspoon each salt and black pepper. Add ½ cup of the pizza sauce and the wine. Mix in the turkey.

5. Spread the turkey mixture evenly over the bottom of the prepared baking dish, pushing it up all around the sides to resemble a crust. Pour half of the pizza sauce onto the turkey crust. Cover with the shredded cheeses. Ladle the remaining sauce over the cheese layer. Place the dish on the upper rack of the oven and bake for 15 minutes. Let stand for 5 minutes before cutting into wedges.

Potato Pie
with Eggs and Cheese

S E R V E S   4

4 SLICES OF BACON

1 MEDIUM ONION, COARSELY CHOPPED

1½ POUNDS SMALL UNPEELED RED
   POTATOES, CUT INTO VERY THIN
   SLICES

5 EGGS

2 TABLESPOONS MILK

½ TEASPOON THYME

½ TEASPOON SALT

¼ TEASPOON BLACK PEPPER

2 TABLESPOONS CHOPPED PARSLEY
   (OPTIONAL)

1 CUP SHREDDED CHEDDAR CHEESE

1. In a large ovenproof skillet, cook the bacon over medium heat until crisp, about 10 minutes. Drain the bacon on paper towels; crumble and set aside. Reserve the fat in the skillet.

2. Preheat the oven to 375°.

3. Add the onion to the fat in the skillet and sauté over medium heat until softened but not browned, about 7 minutes.

4. Add the potato slices and gently toss them with the onion. Increase the heat to medium-high and cook, turning frequently, until the potatoes are tender, about 15 minutes.

5. Meanwhile, in a medium bowl, beat the eggs with the milk, thyme, salt, pepper, and parsley (if using). Stir in the Cheddar.

6. Pour the egg mixture over the potatoes and sprinkle the crumbled bacon on top.

7. Place the skillet in the oven and bake for 8 to 10 minutes, or until the eggs are set. Serve hot, directly from the skillet.

KITCHEN NOTE: *Here's a tip for shredding your own cheese in a food processor: Have the cheese very well chilled, and lightly coat the food processor shredding blade with nonstick cooking spray for easy cleanup. You'll need about 4 ounces of Cheddar to yield 1 cup shredded cheese.*

Tarragon Chicken Pot Pie

SERVES 6

1 CUP CHICKEN BROTH, PREFERABLY
REDUCED-SODIUM

½ POUND UNPEELED RED POTATOES,
CUT INTO ¼-INCH DICE

¾ POUND SKINLESS, BONELESS
CHICKEN BREASTS, DICED

1 LARGE GREEN BELL PEPPER, DICED

2 CELERY RIBS, THINLY SLICED

2 MEDIUM CARROTS, THINLY SLICED

½ POUND SMALL MUSHROOMS

1 CUP FROZEN PEAS

1 TEASPOON TARRAGON

¼ TEASPOON BLACK PEPPER

3 TABLESPOONS FLOUR

3 TABLESPOONS UNSALTED BUTTER, AT
ROOM TEMPERATURE

½ CUP FINE UNSEASONED DRY BREAD
CRUMBS

TWO 9-INCH FROZEN PIE CRUSTS,
THAWED

1 EGG YOLK

1 TABLESPOON MILK

2 TABLESPOONS GRATED PARMESAN
CHEESE

1. Preheat the oven to 425°.

2. In a large skillet, bring the broth to a boil over medium-high heat. Add the potatoes and return to a boil. Cover, reduce the heat to low, and simmer for 9 minutes.

3. Return the broth to a boil over medium-high heat. Add the chicken, bell pepper, celery, carrots, mushrooms, peas, tarragon, and black pepper. Cover the skillet again and return the liquid to a boil.

4. Meanwhile, mix the flour and butter together until completely blended. Bit by bit, stir the flour-butter mixture into the chicken mixture and cook, stirring, until the liquid

thickens and the chicken is cooked through, 3 to 4 minutes. Stir in the bread crumbs. Remove from the heat and let cool slightly.

5. Spoon the filling into one of the pie crusts. Top with the second crust and crimp to seal. Cut slits in the top crust.

6. In a small bowl, stir together the egg yolk and milk. Brush the top crust with the egg-yolk glaze and sprinkle it with the Parmesan.

7. Place the pie on a baking sheet and bake for 15 minutes. Reduce the oven temperature to 325° and bake for 10 minutes, or until the crust is golden.

TURKEY-POTATO SKILLET PIE

SERVES 6

1½ POUNDS SMALL UNPEELED RED
POTATOES

3 GARLIC CLOVES—2 WHOLE AND
1 MINCED

2 TABLESPOONS OLIVE OIL

4 CELERY RIBS, COARSELY CHOPPED

2 MEDIUM ONIONS, COARSELY
CHOPPED

1 MEDIUM GREEN BELL PEPPER,
COARSELY CHOPPED

1 POUND GROUND TURKEY

½ CUP CHICKEN BROTH

1 TEASPOON CORNSTARCH

1 TABLESPOON DIJON MUSTARD

¾ TEASPOON THYME

¼ TEASPOON SALT

½ TEASPOON BLACK PEPPER

2 TABLESPOONS UNSALTED BUTTER

1 EGG, LIGHTLY BEATEN

3 TABLESPOONS GRATED PARMESAN
CHEESE (OPTIONAL)

1. In a large saucepan, combine the potatoes and 2 of the garlic cloves with water to cover. Bring to a boil, cover, and cook until the potatoes are tender, 15 to 18 minutes.

2. Meanwhile, in a large broilerproof skillet, preferably cast-iron, warm the oil over medium-high heat. Add the minced garlic, the celery, onions, and bell pepper, and cook, stirring frequently, until the onions just begin to brown, about 10 minutes.

3. Add the turkey and cook, stirring frequently, until browned, about 5 minutes.

4. In a small bowl, combine the broth, cornstarch, mustard, thyme, salt, and ¼ teaspoon of the black pepper, and stir to blend. Stir the broth mixture into the skillet. Bring the liquid

to a boil, stirring constantly, and cook until the mixture thickens slightly, about 1 minute. Remove from the heat and set aside.

5. Preheat the broiler.

6. Drain the potatoes. In a shallow bowl, mash the potatoes and the garlic. Stir in the butter, beaten egg, remaining ¼ teaspoon black pepper, and the Parmesan (if using). Stir one-third of the potato mixture into the turkey filling.

7. Spoon the remaining mashed potatoes over the turkey mixture in the skillet. Place the pan under the broiler and broil 4 inches from the heat for 10 minutes, or until golden.

Onion and Mushroom Tart

SERVES 4

1 STICK PLUS 3 TABLESPOONS COLD
   UNSALTED BUTTER
1½ CUPS FLOUR
1 TEASPOON SALT
1¾ POUNDS ONIONS, PREFERABLY
   VIDALIA, COARSELY CHOPPED
1½ CUPS QUARTERED MUSHROOMS
1 CUP SLIVERED HAM

½ CUP SHREDDED SWISS CHEESE
3 TABLESPOONS CHOPPED PARSLEY
1 CUP MILK OR HALF-AND-HALF
2 EGG YOLKS
¼ TEASPOON WHITE PEPPER
PINCH OF CAYENNE PEPPER
PINCH OF NUTMEG

1. Cut 1 stick of the butter into small pieces. In a large bowl, combine the flour and salt, and cut in the butter with 2 knives until the mixture is crumbly. Stir in enough cold water (about 2 tablespoons) so that the dough can be gathered into a ball. Wrap in wax paper and chill for 30 minutes.

2. Preheat the oven to 400°.

3. Roll the dough out into an 11-inch circle. Fit the dough into a 9-inch tart pan and trim the edges. Line with foil and fill with dried beans or rice. Bake the shell for 6 to 8 minutes, or until the sides are set. Remove the foil and beans, and return the shell to the oven for about 8 minutes, or until pale gold. Transfer the shell to a rack (leave the oven on).

4. Meanwhile, in a large skillet, combine the onions, 1 tablespoon of the butter, and 1 tablespoon of water. Cover and cook over medium heat until the onions are wilted, about 10 minutes. Uncover and toss until the liquid has evaporated, 1 to 2 minutes. Transfer to a large bowl.

5. Warm the remaining 2 tablespoons butter in the skillet over medium-high heat. Add the mushrooms and sauté until lightly browned, 5 to 7 minutes. Add the mushrooms, ham, cheese, and parsley to the onion mixture in the bowl; toss to combine.

6. In a medium bowl, whisk together the milk, egg yolks, white pepper, cayenne, and nutmeg.

7. Spread the onion mixture in the tart shell; place on the oven rack, and carefully pour the milk mixture on top. Bake for 8 minutes, then lower the heat to 375°. Bake for 25 to 30 minutes, or until the tart is set and lightly golden. Let sit for 5 minutes, then cut into wedges.

Tex-Mex Lattice-Topped Pie

SERVES 8

1¾ CUPS FLOUR

¾ CUP CORNMEAL

½ TEASPOON SALT

6 TABLESPOONS COLD UNSALTED
   BUTTER, CUT INTO PIECES

4 TABLESPOONS COLD SHORTENING

1½ CUPS SHREDDED CHEDDAR CHEESE

ABOUT 6 TABLESPOONS ICE WATER

1 TABLESPOON OLIVE OIL

1 LARGE ONION, COARSELY CHOPPED

4 GARLIC CLOVES, MINCED

1 POUND LEAN GROUND BEEF

2 MEDIUM PICKLED JALAPEÑO PEPPERS,
   MINCED

2 TABLESPOONS CHILI POWDER

2 TEASPOONS CUMIN

1½ TEASPOONS OREGANO

4 LARGE PLUM TOMATOES, COARSELY
   CHOPPED

5 SCALLIONS, COARSELY CHOPPED

1 CUP SHREDDED LETTUCE

½ CUP SOUR CREAM

1. In a large bowl, combine the flour, cornmeal and salt. Cut in the butter and shortening. Stir in 1 cup of the Cheddar cheese. Sprinkle in 4 to 6 tablespoons of the ice water and toss with a fork; the dough should barely hold together. Form the dough into two disks, one twice as large as the other; wrap well and chill while you prepare the filling.

2. In a large skillet, warm the oil over medium-high heat. Add the onion and garlic, and stir-fry for 5 minutes. Crumble in the beef and cook until it is no longer pink, 3 to 5 minutes. Add the jalapeños, chili powder, cumin, and oregano, and cook until fragrant, about 1 minute. Remove from the heat; stir in ⅓ cup each of the tomatoes and scallions.

3. Preheat the oven to 425°. On a floured surface, roll the larger of the two disks of dough into an 11-inch circle. Fit the dough into a 9-inch pie plate and trip the overhang to ½ inch. Roll out the remaining dough into a 10-inch circle and cut the circle into 8 strips.

4. Spoon the filling into the pie shell and sprinkle with the remaining ½ cup Cheddar. Place 4 strips of dough across the pie. Place the remaining 4 strips of dough perpendicular to the first set. Fold the overhang over the ends of the lattice strips and crimp to seal.

5. Bake the pie for 17 to 20 minutes, or until the crust is golden.

6. Serve the pie with the remaining tomatoes and scallions, the lettuce, and sour cream.

SOUTHWEST SALAD BOWL

SERVES 4

◆ EXTRA-QUICK

1 LARGE HEAD OF ROMAINE LETTUCE,
   TORN INTO BITE-SIZE PIECES
2 MEDIUM TOMATOES, DICED
1 MEDIUM GREEN BELL PEPPER, DICED
1 MEDIUM RED BELL PEPPER, DICED
½ MEDIUM AVOCADO, DICED
4 SCALLIONS, FINELY CHOPPED
½ CUP PITTED BLACK OLIVES
½ CUP FROZEN CORN KERNELS,
   THAWED

1 CUP DICED PEPPER JACK CHEESE
ONE 15-OUNCE CAN CHICK-PEAS,
   RINSED AND DRAINED
3 TABLESPOONS FRESH LIME JUICE
1½ TEASPOONS CHILI POWDER
1 TEASPOON GROUND CORIANDER
½ TEASPOON PAPRIKA
¼ TEASPOON SALT
½ CUP OLIVE OIL

1. In a large salad bowl, combine the lettuce, tomatoes, bell peppers, avocado, scallions, olives, corn, cheese, and chick-peas. Toss gently to combine. Cover the bowl with plastic wrap and refrigerate until ready to serve.

2. In a small bowl, combine the lime juice, chili powder, coriander, paprika, and salt; stir with a fork until blended. Beating with the fork, add the oil in a slow, steady stream and continue beating until well blended.

3. Just before serving, stir the dressing to recombine. Pour the dressing over the salad and toss until evenly coated.

VARIATION: *For a more substantial main dish, add grilled chicken. Rub 4 boneless chicken breasts with chili powder and coriander mixed with a little oil; grill or broil until done. Divide the salad among 4 plates. Cut each chicken breast into 5 or 6 diagonal slices and fan 1 sliced chicken breast over each salad.*

Oriental Chicken and Rice Salad

SERVES 6

◆ EXTRA-QUICK

2 CUPS CHICKEN BROTH, PREFERABLY
REDUCED-SODIUM

6 QUARTER-SIZE SLICES FRESH GINGER,
MINCED

¼ TEASPOON RED PEPPER FLAKES

1 CUP RICE

2 GARLIC CLOVES, MINCED

6 TABLESPOONS ORIENTAL (DARK)
SESAME OIL

1¼ POUNDS SKINLESS, BONELESS
CHICKEN BREASTS

¼ CUP ORANGE JUICE

3 TABLESPOONS CIDER VINEGAR

2 TABLESPOONS REDUCED-SODIUM SOY
SAUCE

1 TABLESPOON GRATED ORANGE ZEST

¼ TEASPOON BLACK PEPPER

3 MEDIUM CARROTS, THINLY SLICED
ON THE DIAGONAL

¼ POUND MUSHROOMS, SLICED

¼ POUND SNOW PEAS, SLIVERED

4 SCALLIONS, FINELY CHOPPED

¼ CUP (PACKED) CILANTRO SPRIGS,
FINELY CHOPPED

1. In a medium saucepan, bring the broth, half the ginger, and the red pepper flakes to a boil over medium-high heat, covered. Add the rice, reduce the heat to medium-low, cover, and simmer until the rice is tender and all the liquid is absorbed, about 20 minutes. Set the rice aside, uncovered, to cool slightly.

2. Meanwhile, in a small bowl, combine the remaining ginger with the garlic and 1 table-spoon of the sesame oil.

3. Preheat the broiler. Line a broiler pan with foil.

4. Place the chicken on the prepared broiler pan and brush with half of the ginger-garlic

mixture. Broil the chicken 4 inches from the heat for 6 minutes. Turn the chicken over, brush with the remaining ginger-garlic mixture, and broil for 7 minutes, or until the chicken is cooked through. Slice the chicken across the grain into ¼-inch-wide strips.

5. Meanwhile, in a large salad bowl, combine the orange juice, vinegar, soy sauce, orange zest, pepper, and remaining 5 tablespoons sesame oil.

6. Add the chicken (and any juices from the broiler pan) and rice to the salad bowl. Add the carrots, mushrooms, snow peas, scallions, and cilantro, and toss well. Serve warm.

Mexican Chicken Salad

SERVES 4

♦ EXTRA-QUICK

¼ CUP FRESH LEMON JUICE

2 MEDIUM AVOCADOS

1 GARLIC CLOVE, MINCED

1 TEASPOON DRY MUSTARD

3 TABLESPOONS WHITE WINE VINEGAR

¼ TEASPOON SALT

¼ TEASPOON WHITE PEPPER

½ HEAD OF ICEBERG LETTUCE, SHREDDED

¼ POUND SPINACH, STEMMED AND SHREDDED

2 TABLESPOONS VEGETABLE OIL

1¼ POUNDS SKINLESS, BONELESS CHICKEN BREASTS, CUT INTO 2 x ½-INCH STRIPS

ONE 4-OUNCE CAN WHOLE MILD GREEN CHILIES, CUT INTO THIN STRIPS

¾ CUP SHREDDED MONTEREY JACK CHEESE

2 CUPS TORTILLA CHIPS, CRUMBLED

1. Place the lemon juice in a small bowl. Halve the avocados lengthwise. Using the small end of a melon baller, scoop out the avocado flesh. Add the avocado balls to the lemon juice and toss until evenly coated; set aside.

2. In a small bowl, combine the garlic, mustard, vinegar, salt, and pepper, and stir with a fork to combine; set the vinaigrette aside.

3. Line 4 dinner plates with the lettuce and spinach, and set aside.

4. In a large nonstick skillet, warm the oil over medium-high heat. Add the chicken strips and stir-fry until the chicken is just opaque, 2 to 3 minutes. Add the green chilies and vinaigrette, and stir-fry for 2 minutes.

5. Dividing evenly, spoon the chicken mixture over the greens on the plates. Top with the shredded cheese and garnish each serving with some of the avocado balls and tortilla chips.

Thai Turkey, Shrimp, and Fruit Salad

SERVES 4

◆ EXTRA-QUICK

⅓ CUP FRESH LIME JUICE

¼ CUP ORIENTAL (DARK) SESAME OIL

3 TABLESPOONS HONEY

1 SMALL GARLIC CLOVE, COARSELY CHOPPED

¼ CUP FRESH MINT LEAVES, CHOPPED, OR 1 TEASPOON DRIED

2 TEASPOONS GRATED LIME ZEST

¼ TEASPOON RED PEPPER FLAKES

PINCH OF SALT

½ POUND COOKED TURKEY, CUT INTO ½-INCH CUBES

½ POUND COOKED BABY SHRIMP

1 NAVEL ORANGE, PEELED AND CUT INTO THIN HALF-ROUNDS

2 CUPS PINEAPPLE CHUNKS, FRESH OR CANNED

2 CUPS SEEDLESS RED GRAPES

½ CUP UNSALTED PEANUTS (OPTIONAL)

1. In a large serving bowl, combine the lime juice, sesame oil, honey, garlic, mint, lime zest, red pepper flakes, and salt.

2. Add the turkey, shrimp, orange, pineapple, and grapes to the serving bowl, and toss to coat with the vinaigrette.

3. Serve the salad with the peanuts sprinkled on top, if desired.

Kitchen Note: *This salad can be prepared in advance and refrigerated until serving time. However, because fresh pineapple contains an enzyme that acts as a natural meat tenderizer by breaking down protein (papaya contains a similar enzyme), you'll want to add it at the last minute. Otherwise the pineapple juice will turn the shrimp and turkey mushy. Canned pineapple, on the other hand, doesn't present this problem.*

Turkey Salad with Buttermilk Dressing

SERVES 6

♦ EXTRA-QUICK

1¼ POUNDS SMALL UNPEELED RED
POTATOES

2 TABLESPOONS OLIVE OIL

1 CUP MEDIUM MUSHROOMS,
QUARTERED

⅜ TEASPOON SALT

1 LARGE GREEN BELL PEPPER, CUT INTO
½-INCH PIECES

⅓ CUP DRY WHITE WINE

¼ CUP BUTTERMILK

¼ CUP PLAIN LOW-FAT YOGURT

2 TABLESPOONS RED WINE VINEGAR

1 TABLESPOON FRESH LEMON JUICE

1 GARLIC CLOVE, CHOPPED

½ TEASPOON CELERY SEED

4 DROPS OF HOT PEPPER SAUCE

¼ TEASPOON BLACK PEPPER

1 POUND COOKED TURKEY, CUT INTO
½-INCH CUBES

½ CUP WATERCRESS LEAVES

½ CUP CHOPPED SCALLIONS

1 HEAD OF BIBB LETTUCE, SEPARATED
INTO LEAVES

2 MEDIUM TOMATOES, SLICED

1 SMALL CUCUMBER, SLICED

1 MEDIUM RED ONION, THINLY SLICED

1. In a large pot of boiling water, cook the potatoes, covered, until tender, about 20 minutes. When they are cool enough to handle, cut into ¾-inch cubes. Place in a large bowl.

2. Meanwhile, in a medium skillet, warm the oil over medium heat. Add the mushrooms and ⅛ teaspoon of the salt, and cook for 1 minute. Add the bell pepper and wine, and cook, stirring occasionally, for 5 minutes.

3. In a small bowl, blend the buttermilk, yogurt, vinegar, lemon juice, garlic, celery seed,

hot pepper sauce, remaining ¼ teaspoon salt, and the black pepper. Set aside.

4. Add the turkey, watercress, and scallions to the potatoes in the bowl. Add the sautéed vegetables and toss to combine.

5. Add the dressing to the turkey mixture and toss lightly. Arrange the lettuce on individual plates and place a generous portion of the salad on each. Garnish with the tomatoes, cucumber, and red onion.

Turkey and Black Bean Salad

SERVES 4 TO 6

♦ EXTRA-QUICK

¼ POUND SNOW PEAS, SLIVERED

6 TABLESPOONS RED WINE VINEGAR

2 TABLESPOONS FRESH LEMON JUICE

1 TABLESPOON DIJON MUSTARD

1 TABLESPOON HONEY

5 DROPS OF HOT PEPPER SAUCE

3 TABLESPOONS CHOPPED CILANTRO

2 GARLIC CLOVES, CHOPPED

½ TEASPOON FRESH THYME, OR
   ¼ TEASPOON DRIED

⅛ TEASPOON SALT

⅛ TEASPOON BLACK PEPPER

⅓ CUP OLIVE OIL

½ SMALL CANTALOUPE, PEELED AND
   CUT INTO SMALL CHUNKS

3 SCALLIONS, FINELY SLICED

1 LARGE TOMATO, COARSELY CHOPPED

1 SMALL GREEN BELL PEPPER, CHOPPED

1 SMALL ONION, COARSELY CHOPPED

1¾ POUNDS COOKED TURKEY, CUT
   INTO THIN STRIPS

ONE 16-OUNCE CAN BLACK BEANS,
   RINSED AND DRAINED

1 HEAD OF BIBB LETTUCE, SEPARATED
   INTO LEAVES

1. In a small saucepan of boiling water, blanch the snow peas for 15 seconds. Drain and rinse under cold running water. Set aside.

2. In a food processor or blender, combine the vinegar, lemon juice, mustard, honey, hot pepper sauce, cilantro, garlic, thyme, salt, and black pepper, and process for 15 seconds. With the machine running, add the oil in a slow, steady stream and process until smooth, about 30 seconds.

3. In a large bowl, combine the cantaloupe, scallions, tomato, bell pepper, onion, and turkey. Add the snow peas and black beans. Pour 1 cup of the dressing over the salad and toss lightly.

4. To serve, arrange the lettuce leaves on a platter or on individual plates, and mound the salad on the lettuce. Pass the remaining dressing.

Smoked Turkey and Pistachio Rice Salad

SERVES 4

½ CUP RICE

½ POUND FULLY COOKED SMOKED
   SAUSAGE, CUT INTO ¼-INCH SLICES

⅓ CUP UNSALTED, SHELLED PISTACHIO
   NUTS

4 TABLESPOONS OLIVE OIL

2 TABLESPOONS WHITE WINE VINEGAR

½ TEASPOON DRY MUSTARD

¼ TEASPOON SALT

¼ TEASPOON BLACK PEPPER

ONE 10-OUNCE PACKAGE FROZEN
   CORN KERNELS, THAWED

6 SCALLIONS, THINLY SLICED

¾ POUND SMOKED TURKEY BREAST,
   CUT INTO ½-INCH-WIDE STRIPS

1 BUNCH OF WATERCRESS, LARGE
   STEMS TRIMMED

1. In a medium covered saucepan, bring 1 cup of water to a boil over medium-high heat. Add the rice, reduce the heat to low, cover, and simmer until the rice is tender and the water is absorbed, 15 to 20 minutes. Remove the rice from the heat and fluff it with a fork. Spread the rice out on a platter, cover with plastic wrap, and place in the freezer to chill.

2. Preheat the oven to 350°.

3. Place the sausage lengthwise on a large, rectangular sheet of foil. Gather the long edges together, and fold twice to seal; repeat with the short ends to seal. Place the packets on a baking sheet. Place the pistachios next to the packets and bake both for 10 minutes. Remove the baking sheet from the oven, open the packets, and set aside to cool.

4. Meanwhile, in a small bowl, blend 3 tablespoons of the oil with the vinegar, mustard, salt, and pepper; set aside.

5. In a medium skillet, warm the remaining 1 tablespoon oil over medium-high heat. Add the corn and scallions, and sauté, stirring, until the scallions are softened, 1 to 2 minutes. Remove from the heat and set aside to cool.

6. In a large bowl, combine the chilled rice, corn and scallion mixture, roasted nuts, and vinaigrette, and toss well to combine.

7. Divide the rice mixture among 4 dinner plates. Top each serving with equal portions of the baked sausage and turkey strips. Arrange the watercress around the rice.

Lemon-Marinated Fish and Pasta Salad

SERVES 4

◇ LOW-FAT

1 POUND SWORDFISH, HALIBUT, OR
    MAHI-MAHI, CUT INTO 2-INCH
    PIECES

¼ CUP PLUS 1 TABLESPOON FRESH
    LEMON JUICE

1 TABLESPOON CHOPPED FRESH THYME,
    OR 1 TEASPOON DRIED

⅛ TEASPOON CAYENNE PEPPER

¼ TEASPOON SALT

½ TEASPOON BLACK PEPPER

4 SCALLIONS, SLICED

1 MEDIUM CARROT, CUT INTO
    MATCHSTICKS

1 CELERY RIB, CUT INTO MATCHSTICKS

½ TEASPOON DIJON MUSTARD

1 TABLESPOON MINCED FRESH DILL, OR
    2 TEASPOONS DRIED

2 TABLESPOONS OLIVE OIL

½ POUND LINGUINE, PREFERABLY A
    MIXTURE OF SPINACH AND REGULAR

1. Place the fish pieces in a shallow dish. In a small bowl, combine ¼ cup of the lemon juice, the thyme, cayenne, salt, and ¼ teaspoon of the black pepper. Pour the lemon marinade over the fish and let the fish marinate in the refrigerator for 30 minutes.

2. Meanwhile, in a medium bowl, toss the scallions, carrot, and celery with ⅛ teaspoon of the black pepper; set aside.

3. In a small bowl, combine the mustard, dill, and the remaining 1 tablespoon lemon juice and ⅛ teaspoon black pepper. Whisk in the oil in a thin, steady stream; set aside.

4. In a large pot of boiling water, cook the linguine until al dente according to package directions. Drain the pasta and rinse it under cold running water, then transfer it to a large bowl and toss it with half of the dressing.

5. In a steamer insert large enough to hold the vegetables and the fish, steam the vegetables over 1 inch of boiling water for 1 minute. Place the fish on top and steam until the fish is opaque, 1 to 2 minutes. Remove the steamer and let the fish and vegetables cool.

6. To serve, mound the pasta on a platter, spoon the fish and vegetables on top, and pour the remaining dressing over the salad.

Shrimp Salad with Curry Sauce

SERVES 4

◆ EXTRA-QUICK

½ POUND MEDIUM SHRIMP

⅔ CUP SOUR CREAM

⅓ CUP MAYONNAISE

2 TEASPOONS CURRY POWDER

¼ TEASPOON SALT

¼ TEASPOON BLACK PEPPER

4 HARD-COOKED EGGS, THINLY SLICED

1 LARGE GRANNY SMITH APPLE, DICED

4 PICKLED HERRING FILLETS, CUT INTO
  1-INCH-WIDE PIECES

ONE 8-OUNCE CAN SLICED BEETS,
  RINSED AND DRAINED

½ POUND MUSHROOMS, THINLY SLICED

1 MEDIUM CUCUMBER, THINLY SLICED

1 MEDIUM RED ONION, THINLY SLICED

1. In a medium saucepan of boiling water, cook the shrimp until just opaque, 3 to 4 minutes. Drain in a colander and rinse under cold running water. Shell and devein the shrimp and set aside to cool.

2. In a small bowl, combine the sour cream, mayonnaise, curry powder, salt, and pepper, and stir until well blended. Set aside.

3. Divide the shrimp, eggs, apple, herring, beets, mushrooms, cucumber, and onion among 4 dinner plates, arranging them in an attractive pattern. Serve with the curry sauce on the side.

Variation: *Instead of serving this Scandinavian-style salad as a main dish, use its components as part of a crowd-pleasing buffet— what the Swedish call a smörgåsbord. Present the shrimp, eggs, apple, herring, beets, mushrooms, cucumber, and onion on separate platters, and fill out the meal with sliced smoked salmon, smoked whitefish, thinly sliced roast beef and ham, and a selection of mustards. Serve with party pumpernickel and rye bread.*

SHRIMP AND PASTA WITH SPINACH PESTO

SERVES 4

6 WHOLE BLACK PEPPERCORNS

½ MEDIUM ONION, COARSELY CHOPPED

½ TEASPOON THYME

2 BAY LEAVES

1 CUP TARRAGON VINEGAR

2 CUPS DRY WHITE WINE

¾ POUND FUSILLI OR LINGUINE

1½ POUNDS MEDIUM SHRIMP, SHELLED AND DEVEINED

1 POUND FRESH SPINACH, STEMMED AND CUT INTO ½-INCH-WIDE STRIPS

4 GARLIC CLOVES, MINCED

¾ CUP (PACKED) SHREDDED FRESH BASIL

½ CUP GRATED PARMESAN CHEESE

¾ CUP OLIVE OIL

ONE 10-OUNCE PACKAGE FROZEN PEAS, THAWED

¼ TEASPOON SALT

¼ TEASPOON BLACK PEPPER

1. Crack the peppercorns under the blade of a large knife. In a large nonaluminum saucepan, combine the peppercorns, onion, thyme, bay leaves, vinegar, wine, and 8 cups of cold water. Bring to a boil, partially covered, over high heat. Reduce the heat to medium-high; simmer the poaching liquid for 15 minutes.

2. Meanwhile, in a large pot of boiling water, cook the pasta until al dente according to package directions. Drain, rinse under cold running water, and drain again. Set aside.

3. Add the shrimp to the poaching liquid and cook until just opaque, about 5 minutes. Reserving the poaching liquid, transfer the shrimp to a plate and set aside to cool.

4. Place the spinach in a strainer, then dip the strainer into the poaching liquid just long enough to wilt the spinach. Set the spinach aside to cool. (Reserve the poaching liquid for another use or discard.)

5. Squeeze the spinach to remove excess moisture and transfer to a food processor or blender. Add the garlic, basil, Parmesan, and olive oil to the spinach, and purée.

6. In a large bowl, combine the pasta, peas, salt, and pepper, and toss to combine. Add half the spinach pesto and toss well. Divide the pasta mixture among 4 bowls and top with the shrimp. Serve with the remaining spinach pesto on the side.

SHRIMP AND VEGETABLE RICE SALAD

SERVES 4

2 CUPS RICE

1¼ POUNDS LARGE SHRIMP, SHELLED
AND DEVEINED

1 MEDIUM CARROT, CUT INTO LONG
MATCHSTICKS

½ CUP SUGAR

1½ TEASPOONS SALT

½ POUND SMALL MUSHROOMS

5 TABLESPOONS DISTILLED WHITE
VINEGAR

1 TEASPOON DRY WHITE WINE

⅓ CUP MAYONNAISE

2 TEASPOONS REDUCED-SODIUM SOY
SAUCE

1 TABLESPOON KETCHUP

HOT PEPPER SAUCE

ONE 8-OUNCE CAN SLICED WATER
CHESTNUTS, RINSED AND DRAINED

ONE 10-OUNCE PACKAGE FROZEN
PEAS, THAWED

¼ CUP WALNUTS OR ALMONDS,
COARSELY CHOPPED

1. In medium covered saucepan, bring 3½ cups of water to a boil over high heat. Add the rice, reduce the heat, cover, and simmer until the rice is tender, about 20 minutes. Fluff the rice into a large bowl to cool.

2. Meanwhile, cook the shrimp in a large saucepan of boiling water until they turn opaque, about 5 minutes. One minute before the shrimp are done, add the carrot. Drain the shrimp and carrot, and rinse under cold running water; set aside to cool.

3. In a medium saucepan, bring 3 cups of water, ¼ cup of the sugar, and 1 teaspoon of the salt to a boil. Add the mushrooms and stir. Reduce the heat, cover, and simmer for 5 minutes. Drain and rinse under cold running water. Drain the mushrooms on paper towels.

4. In a small bowl, combine the vinegar, wine, and the remaining ¼ cup sugar and ½ teaspoon salt, and whisk until blended.

5. In another small bowl, combine the mayonnaise, soy sauce, ketchup, and a dash of hot pepper sauce, and stir until blended.

6. Add the mushrooms, carrot, water chestnuts, and vinaigrette to the rice, and toss gently. Divide the mixture among 4 dinner plates and sprinkle with the peas. Arrange the shrimp around the border of each plate. Sprinkle with the nuts and serve the spicy mayonnaise on the side.

CRAB SALAD WITH SPINACH AND CORN

SERVES 4

◇ LOW - FAT

½ POUND FRESH SPINACH, STEMMED

1 CUP FROZEN CORN KERNELS, THAWED

1 POUND LUMP CRABMEAT, PICKED OVER

1 LARGE TOMATO, CHOPPED

2 TABLESPOONS WHITE WINE VINEGAR

1 TABLESPOON CREAM SHERRY

1 GARLIC CLOVE, MINCED

¾ TEASPOON DIJON MUSTARD

¼ CUP PLAIN LOW-FAT YOGURT

1½ TEASPOONS SOUR CREAM

⅛ TEASPOON SALT

PINCH OF WHITE PEPPER

PINCH OF CAYENNE PEPPER

1 HEAD OF RED LEAF LETTUCE, SEPARATED INTO LEAVES

1. Wash the spinach and place it, with just the water that clings to its leaves, in a pot. Cover the pot and steam the spinach over medium heat until it wilts, 2 to 3 minutes. Drain the spinach; when it is cool enough to handle, squeeze it to remove excess liquid, and chop the spinach coarsely.

2. In a large bowl, combine the spinach, corn, crabmeat, tomato, and vinegar. Cover the bowl and refrigerate for 30 minutes.

3. Meanwhile, in a small bowl, whisk together the sherry, garlic, mustard, yogurt, sour cream, salt, white pepper, and cayenne. Pour the dressing over the crab salad and toss well. Arrange the lettuce leaves on a serving platter, then mound the salad on the leaves.

SUBSTITUTION: *Lump crabmeat can be expensive, so you might want to make this salad with fish instead of shellfish. Try baked or poached halibut, haddock, cod, or salmon, broken into large chunks. Even canned pink salmon would make a tasty salad.*

Cold Beef Salad
with Ginger Dressing

SERVES 4

◆ EXTRA - QUICK

2 GARLIC CLOVES, MINCED

2 TEASPOONS MINCED FRESH GINGER

1 TABLESPOON SUGAR

1 TABLESPOON RICE WINE VINEGAR OR
WHITE WINE VINEGAR

1 TABLESPOON REDUCED-SODIUM SOY
SAUCE

1 TABLESPOON ORIENTAL (DARK)
SESAME OIL

1 TABLESPOON VEGETABLE OIL,
PREFERABLY PEANUT

2 CELERY RIBS, CUT ON THE DIAGONAL
INTO ½-INCH SLICES

3 BUNCHES OF SCALLIONS, CUT INTO
3-INCH PIECES

1½ POUNDS THINLY SLICED RARE
ROAST BEEF, CUT INTO ¼-INCH-
WIDE STRIPS

1 SMALL RED BELL PEPPER, CUT INTO
THIN STRIPS

2 TABLESPOONS SESAME SEEDS,
TOASTED

1. In a small bowl, combine the garlic, ginger, sugar, vinegar, and soy sauce. Whisking constantly, gradually add the sesame and vegetable oils, and stir until blended; set aside.

2. In a medium saucepan of boiling water, blanch the celery for 2 minutes, then add the scallions and blanch for 15 seconds. Drain the celery and scallions in a colander, rinse under cold running water, and drain well.

3. In a shallow serving bowl or on a platter, combine the beef, bell pepper, celery, and scallions, and toss to combine.

4. Whisk the dressing to recombine. Pour the dressing over the salad and toss until evenly coated. Sprinkle with the toasted sesame seeds and serve.

Spicy Pork and Rice Salad

SERVES 6

1½ CUPS BROWN RICE

2 TABLESPOONS PLUS 1 TEASPOON
OLIVE OIL

1 LARGE ONION, THINLY SLICED

1 GARLIC CLOVE, MINCED

1 JALAPEÑO PEPPER, SEEDED AND
MINCED

¾ POUND PORK TENDERLOIN, CUT
INTO ½-INCH CUBES

¼ POUND SKINLESS, BONELESS
CHICKEN BREAST, CUT INTO ½-INCH
CUBES

½ TEASPOON TURMERIC

½ TEASPOON PAPRIKA

¼ TEASPOON CAYENNE PEPPER

2 TABLESPOONS PLUS 1 TEASPOON
REDUCED-SODIUM SOY SAUCE

1 LARGE TOMATO, CUT INTO THIN
SLIVERS

6 OUNCES COOKED SHRIMP

1 EGG

1. In a large saucepan of boiling water, cook the brown rice, covered, until it is tender, about 40 minutes. Drain, rinse under cold running water, and drain well. Set aside.

2. Meanwhile, in a large skillet, warm 2 tablespoons of the oil over medium heat. Add the onion, garlic, and jalapeño, and cook, stirring frequently, for 3 minutes. Add the pork and chicken, and cook, stirring, for 4 minutes.

3. Add the turmeric, paprika, and cayenne, and mix well, then stir in the rice and cook, stirring, for 4 minutes. Add 2 tablespoons of the soy sauce, the tomato, and half of the shrimp, and cook until heated through, about 2 minutes. Transfer the mixture to a serving

platter and cover loosely with foil to keep warm while you make the omelet.

4. In a bowl, beat the egg with the remaining 1 teaspoon soy sauce. In a 6- to 7-inch skillet, warm the remaining 1 teaspoon oil over medium-low heat. Add the egg mixture and tilt the pan to cover the bottom evenly. Cook until the omelet is set, 45 seconds to 1 minute. Loosen the omelet from the pan and turn it out onto a board, then roll up the omelet and cut it crosswise into thin slices.

5. Arrange the omelet slices around the edge of the rice mixture. Garnish with the remaining shrimp and serve hot.

TOMATO AND MELON
SALAD WITH SMOKED HAM

SERVES 4

◆ EXTRA-QUICK

1 LARGE CANTALOUPE

1 LARGE HONEYDEW MELON

⅓ CUP OLIVE OIL

2 TABLESPOONS FRESH LEMON JUICE

¼ TEASPOON SALT

2 TABLESPOONS CHOPPED FRESH BASIL,
   OR 1 TEASPOON DRIED

2 TABLESPOONS MINCED CHIVES

1 PINT CHERRY TOMATOES, HALVED

2 HEADS OF RED LEAF LETTUCE,
   SEPARATED INTO LEAVES

1 POUND THINLY SLICED SMOKED HAM,
   SUCH AS BLACK FOREST

1. Halve the cantaloupe and honeydew; remove and discard seeds. Using large end of a melon baller, carefully scoop out melon balls.

2. In a large bowl, combine the oil, lemon juice, salt, basil, and chives. Add the melon balls and tomato halves, and toss until evenly coated. Cover the bowl and let stand at room temperature for 30 minutes.

3. Divide the lettuce among 4 large plates and top with the melon and tomatoes. Roll up each slice of ham and arrange the slices around the salad.

KITCHEN NOTE: *This unexpected combination of fruit and vegetables will, of course, taste best with the sweetest possible cantaloupe and honeydew. Look for a cantaloupe that's golden (not greenish); the scar at the stem end should be sunken, and you should be able to sniff a light floral fragrance at that spot. A honeydew should be creamy yellow, its skin velvety rather than slick. Large honeydews are usually sweetest.*

Smoked Ham and Spinach Salad

SERVES 4

¾ POUND SMALL UNPEELED RED
    POTATOES, THINLY SLICED

1 POUND FRESH SPINACH, STEMMED
    AND TORN INTO BITE-SIZE PIECES

¾ CUP REDUCED-FAT MAYONNAISE

4 TEASPOONS DIJON MUSTARD

2 TABLESPOONS HALF-AND-HALF

2 TABLESPOONS CHOPPED FRESH
    TARRAGON, OR ¼ TEASPOON DRIED

1 TABLESPOON CHOPPED CHIVES OR
    SCALLION GREENS

¾ POUND THINLY SLICED MILD
    SMOKED HAM, SUCH AS
    WESTPHALIAN

¼ TEASPOON BLACK PEPPER

2 TABLESPOONS CHOPPED PARSLEY

1. In a medium saucepan, combine the potatoes with cold water to cover and bring to a boil over high heat. Reduce the heat to medium and cook, uncovered, until the potatoes are tender, 10 to 15 minutes. Drain well and set aside to cool.

2. Meanwhile, line 4 plates with the spinach and set aside.

3. In a small bowl, combine the mayonnaise, mustard, half-and-half, tarragon, and chives, and stir with a fork until blended; set aside.

4. Loosely roll each slice of ham into a cone shape and arrange the slices in the center of each spinach-lined plate. Place the potatoes on both sides of the ham and sprinkle with the pepper.

5. Drizzle each salad with some of the mayonnaise dressing, sprinkle with the parsley, and serve the remaining dressing on the side.

Ham, Vegetable, and Noodle Salad

SERVES 4

♦ EXTRA-QUICK

1 POUND FRESH CHINESE EGG
  NOODLES, OR ¾ POUND DRIED
  CAPELLINI OR SPAGHETTINI
¾ CUP GRANULATED SUGAR
¾ TEASPOON SALT
½ TEASPOON BLACK PEPPER
½ CUP DISTILLED WHITE VINEGAR
2 TABLESPOONS FRESH LEMON JUICE
½ CUP VEGETABLE OIL
½ POUND FRESH SPINACH, STEMMED

1 MEDIUM CUCUMBER, CUT INTO LONG
  MATCHSTICKS
1 MEDIUM ZUCCHINI, CUT INTO LONG
  MATCHSTICKS
1 LARGE RED ONION—HALVED, THINLY
  SLICED, AND SEPARATED INTO STRIPS
1 PINT CHERRY TOMATOES
1¼ POUNDS DANISH HAM, CUT INTO
  MATCHSTICKS

1. In a large pot of boiling water, cook the noodles until al dente according to package directions. Drain in a colander, rinse under cold running water, and drain well. Set aside.

2. Meanwhile, in a small bowl, combine the sugar, salt, pepper, vinegar, and lemon juice, and stir with a fork until blended. Beating with the fork, add the oil in a slow, steady stream and beat until blended. Set aside.

3. Divide the spinach among 4 dinner plates. Divide the noodles among the plates, mounding them in the center. Top the noodles with the cucumber, zucchini, and onion. Arrange the cherry tomatoes and ham strips decoratively around noodles.

4. Just before serving, stir the dressing to recombine and spoon over the salads.

Hoppin' John Salad

SERVES 4

◆ EXTRA-QUICK

½ CUP RICE

ONE 10-OUNCE PACKAGE FROZEN
   BLACK-EYED PEAS

4 PLUM TOMATOES OR 2 MEDIUM
   TOMATOES, COARSELY CHOPPED

3 CELERY RIBS, COARSELY CHOPPED

1 LARGE YELLOW OR RED BELL PEPPER,
   COARSELY CHOPPED

6 SCALLIONS, COARSELY CHOPPED

3 TABLESPOONS FRESH LEMON JUICE

1 TABLESPOON YELLOW MUSTARD

1 GARLIC CLOVE, MINCED

4 TEASPOONS GRATED LEMON ZEST

½ TEASPOON BLACK PEPPER

⅓ CUP OLIVE OIL

½ POUND SMOKED HAM, CUT INTO
   ¼-INCH DICE

1. In a medium saucepan, bring 1 cup of water, the rice, and black-eyed peas to a boil over medium-high heat. Reduce the heat to medium-low, cover, and simmer until the rice and black-eyed peas are tender and all the liquid is absorbed, 15 to 20 minutes. Remove from the heat and set aside to cool slightly.

2. Meanwhile, in a large bowl, combine the tomatoes, celery, bell pepper, and scallions.

3. In a small bowl, combine the lemon juice, mustard, garlic, lemon zest, and black pepper. Whisk in the olive oil until well blended.

4. Add the rice and black-eyed peas to the vegetables. Add the ham and dressing, and toss to combine.

SWEET AFTERTHOUGHT: *Hoppin' John, which inspired this salad, is a Southern dish made by cooking black-eyed peas and rice with bacon or ham. Follow the salad with a variation on another Southern classic—ambrosia sundaes. Peel and chop 2 navel oranges and toss with 1 cup drained crushed pineapple and 1 diced banana. Spoon this mixture over scoops of vanilla ice cream and top with ¼ cup sweetened shredded coconut that's been briefly skillet-toasted.*

CREOLE-STYLE
POTATO SALAD WITH SAUSAGE

SERVES 4

2 POUNDS SMALL UNPEELED RED
  POTATOES
½ CUP MINCED RED ONION
½ CUP MINCED SCALLIONS
¼ CUP MINCED PARSLEY
6 TABLESPOONS CIDER VINEGAR
4 ROMAINE LETTUCE LEAVES
½ CUP OLIVE OIL
½ POUND KIELBASA OR OTHER FULLY
  COOKED GARLIC SAUSAGE, COARSELY
  CHOPPED

1 GARLIC CLOVE, MINCED
1 TABLESPOON CREOLE OR DIJON
  MUSTARD
½ TEASPOON BLACK PEPPER
¼ TEASPOON CAYENNE PEPPER
HOT PEPPER SAUCE

1. In a medium saucepan of boiling water, cook the potatoes until tender, 20 to 30 minutes. Drain in a colander and set aside to cool. When they are cool enough to handle, halve them and then cut into ¼-inch-thick slices.

2. In a large bowl, combine the potatoes, onion, scallions, and parsley, and sprinkle with 3 tablespoons of the cider vinegar.

3. Line a serving platter with the Romaine lettuce and set aside.

4. In a medium skillet, warm the oil over medium heat. Add the sausage and sauté, stirring, until browned, about 5 minutes. Remove the pan from the heat and, reserving the fat in the pan, transfer sausage to paper towels to drain. Add sausage to the potato mixture.

5. To the fat remaining in the pan, add the garlic, mustard, black pepper, cayenne, remaining 3 tablespoons vinegar, and hot pepper sauce to taste, and bring to a boil, whisking constantly, over medium-high heat.

6. Pour the hot vinaigrette over the potato salad and toss gently to combine. Spoon over the lettuce on the platter and serve warm.

BLT in a Bowl

SERVES 4

◆ EXTRA-QUICK

½ POUND BACON, CUT CROSSWISE
INTO 1-INCH-WIDE PIECES

4 TABLESPOONS FRESH LEMON JUICE

1 LARGE GARLIC CLOVE, LIGHTLY
CRUSHED AND PEELED

¾ CUP VEGETABLE OIL

1 SMALL HEAD OF ROMAINE LETTUCE,
SEPARATED INTO LEAVES

1 SMALL HEAD OF ICEBERG LETTUCE,
SEPARATED INTO LEAVES

1 PINT CHERRY TOMATOES, HALVED

½ POUND JARLSBERG CHEESE,
SHREDDED

½ CUP GRATED PARMESAN CHEESE

½ CUP SLIVERED ALMONDS, TOASTED

¼ TEASPOON SALT

¼ TEASPOON BLACK PEPPER

1 LOAF ITALIAN BREAD, SLICED

I. In a medium skillet, cook the bacon over medium-high heat until crisp, about 8 minutes. Drain on paper towels and set aside.

2. In a small bowl, combine the lemon juice and whole garlic. Beating with a fork, add the oil in a slow, steady stream and beat until well blended. Set aside until ready to serve.

3. Gather the lettuce leaves into stacks and cut crosswise into ½-inch-wide shreds. Place lettuce in a large salad bowl. Add the bacon, tomatoes, cheeses, and almonds, and toss to combine.

4. Beat the dressing to recombine, then remove and discard the garlic. Add the dressing to the salad and toss until evenly coated. Add the salt and pepper, and serve the salad with the bread on the side.

KITCHEN NOTE: *Trim some calories (and save some time) by substituting reduced-fat or nonfat mayonnaise for the vinaigrette in this recipe. Use ½ cup of mayonnaise thinned with lemon juice (2 or 3 tablespoons) and seasoned with 1 teaspoon of very finely minced garlic. Using reduced-fat Jarlsberg cheese, which is widely available, would further help to cut the fat.*

HEARTY VEGETABLE CHOWDER

SERVES 4

½ POUND THICK-SLICED BACON, CUT
CROSSWISE INTO ½-INCH PIECES

3 MEDIUM ONIONS, DICED

3 MEDIUM CARROTS, SLICED

2 MEDIUM CELERY RIBS, SLICED

1½ POUNDS ALL-PURPOSE POTATOES,
PEELED AND DICED

3 CUPS CHICKEN BROTH, PREFERABLY
REDUCED-SODIUM

½ TEASPOON SALT

½ TEASPOON BLACK PEPPER

PINCH OF THYME

1½ CUPS SMALL BROCCOLI FLORETS

¾ CUP GREEN BEANS, HALVED

2 MEDIUM RED BELL PEPPERS, DICED

1 MEDIUM ZUCCHINI, SLICED

1 CUP SLICED MUSHROOMS

¾ CUP CANNED NO-SALT-ADDED
WHOLE TOMATOES, CHOPPED AND
DRAINED

½ CUP CORN KERNELS, FRESH OR
FROZEN

½ CUP PEAS, FRESH OR FROZEN

⅔ CUP HALF-AND-HALF

½ CUP MILK

1. In a large pot, cook the bacon over medium-low heat until golden but not crisp. Transfer to paper towels to drain; set aside. Pour off all but 2 tablespoons of the fat.

2. Add the onions, carrots, and celery to the bacon fat in the pot, increase the heat to medium, and sauté until the onions are softened, about 8 minutes.

3. Add the potatoes, broth, salt, black pepper, and thyme, and stir to combine. Bring to a simmer and cook until the potatoes are tender, about 15 minutes. With a slotted spoon, transfer about half of the vegetables to a food processor or blender; set aside.

4. Add the broccoli, green beans, bell peppers, and zucchini to the pot. Simmer until the broccoli is just tender. Meanwhile, purée the vegetables in the food processor or blender until smooth.

5. Return the purée to the soup; add the mushrooms, tomatoes, corn, and peas. Stir in the half-and-half, milk, and bacon, and simmer, stirring occasionally, until the flavors are blended, about 5 minutes. Serve hot.

Minestrone

SERVES 4

¼ POUND LEAN BACON, MINCED

1 MEDIUM CARROT, DICED

1 MEDIUM CELERY RIB, DICED

1 SMALL ONION, DICED

1 MEDIUM ZUCCHINI, THINLY SLICED

1 MEDIUM YELLOW SQUASH, THINLY
SLICED

¼ TEASPOON SALT

¼ TEASPOON BLACK PEPPER

1 CUP SHREDDED SAVOY CABBAGE

ONE 16-OUNCE CAN NO-SALT-ADDED
WHOLE TOMATOES

2 TABLESPOONS FRESH OREGANO, OR
2 TEASPOONS DRIED

1 TABLESPOON CHOPPED FRESH THYME,
OR 1 TEASPOON DRIED

2½ CUPS BEEF BROTH, OR 1¼ CUPS
EACH CHICKEN AND BEEF BROTH

¼ POUND ELBOW MACARONI OR OTHER
SMALL PASTA

½ CUP GRATED ROMANO CHEESE

1. In a large saucepan, cook the bacon over medium heat until crisp, about 10 minutes. Pour off all but 2 tablespoons of the fat.

2. Add the carrot, celery, and onion to the bacon in the pan. Cook, stirring frequently, until the vegetables are softened but not browned, about 7 minutes.

3. Stir in the zucchini, yellow squash, salt, and pepper, and cook for 5 minutes.

4. Stir in the cabbage and cook just until wilted, about 2 minutes. Add the tomatoes, oregano, and thyme, and break up the toma-

toes with the back of a spoon. Add the broth, bring to a boil, reduce the heat to low, and simmer, stirring occasionally, for 25 minutes.

5. Add the pasta and simmer, partially covered, until the pasta is al dente according to package directions.

6. Serve the soup with the grated cheese on the side.

HERBED COUNTRY CHICKEN STEW

SERVES 4

♦ EXTRA-QUICK ◇ LOW-FAT

2½ CUPS CHICKEN BROTH, PREFERABLY REDUCED-SODIUM

1 MEDIUM ONION, CUT INTO THIN WEDGES

3 GARLIC CLOVES, MINCED

1 TEASPOON BASIL

1 TEASPOON THYME

½ TEASPOON OREGANO

¼ TEASPOON BLACK PEPPER

1 BAY LEAF

3 MEDIUM CARROTS, CUT INTO 1-INCH LENGTHS

2 CELERY RIBS, CUT INTO 1-INCH LENGTHS

1 POUND UNPEELED RED POTATOES, CUT INTO ¾-INCH CHUNKS

3 TABLESPOONS UNSALTED BUTTER

3 TABLESPOONS FLOUR

1¼ POUNDS SKINLESS, BONELESS CHICKEN BREASTS, CUT INTO ¾-INCH CHUNKS

¼ CUP CHOPPED PARSLEY (OPTIONAL)

1. In a large saucepan, combine the broth, onion, garlic, basil, thyme, oregano, pepper, and bay leaf, and bring the mixture to a boil over medium-high heat.

2. Add the carrots, celery, and potatoes, and let the broth return to a boil. Reduce the heat to low, cover, and simmer until the potatoes are tender, about 20 minutes.

3. Meanwhile, in a small bowl, thoroughly blend the butter and flour to make a smooth paste.

4. Add the chicken to the simmering broth. Stir in 2 tablespoons of the parsley (if using). Pinch off several pieces of the butter-flour mixture at a time, add them to the simmering broth, and stir well. Repeat until all of the mixture has been incorporated. Cover and cook until the sauce is thickened and the chicken is cooked through, 5 to 7 minutes.

5. Remove and discard the bay leaf. Serve the stew garnished with the remaining chopped parsley (if using).

Shrimp Creole

SERVES 4

◇ LOW-FAT

4 TEASPOONS OLIVE OIL

1 LARGE ONION, THINLY SLICED

2 GARLIC CLOVES, MINCED

1 TABLESPOON FLOUR

1 TABLESPOON CHILI POWDER

1¼ POUNDS LARGE SHRIMP, SHELLED
AND DEVEINED, SHELLS RESERVED

1 CUP VERMOUTH

½ CUP RICE

3 GREEN BELL PEPPERS, CUT INTO THIN
STRIPS

1 LARGE CELERY RIB, THINLY SLICED
ON THE DIAGONAL

1½ POUNDS FRESH TOMATOES,
COARSELY CHOPPED, OR ONE
16-OUNCE CAN NO-SALT-ADDED
WHOLE TOMATOES, COARSELY
CHOPPED

¼ TEASPOON FILÉ POWDER (OPTIONAL)

¼ TEASPOON SALT

1 OUNCE LEAN HAM, JULIENNED
(OPTIONAL)

1. In a large pot, warm 2 teaspoons of the oil over medium heat. Add the onion and sauté until browned, 8 to 10 minutes. Transfer half of the onion to a plate and set aside.

2. Add the garlic to the pot and cook, stirring, for 1 minute. Stir in the flour and chili powder. Add the shrimp shells, vermouth, and 1 cup of water. Bring the liquid to a simmer; reduce the heat to medium-low, cover, and cook the mixture for 20 minutes.

3. Meanwhile, in a medium saucepan, bring 1 cup of water to a boil over high heat. Add the rice, stir once, cover, and reduce the heat to low. Simmer until the rice is tender and the liquid is absorbed, about 20 minutes. Set the rice aside while you finish the stew.

4. In a large skillet, warm the remaining 2 teaspoons oil over medium-high heat. Add the shrimp and sauté, stirring, for 2 minutes. Stir in the bell peppers and celery, and cook for 1 minute. Add the tomatoes, the reserved onion, and the filé powder (if using).

5. Strain the vermouth mixture into the skillet and add the rice. Reduce the heat to low and gently simmer the stew for 5 minutes. Stir in the salt. Garnish the stew with the ham (if using) just before serving.

Chicken Drumsticks Cacciatore

SERVES 6

12 CHICKEN DRUMSTICKS (ABOUT
    4½ POUNDS TOTAL)
¼ TEASPOON SALT
¼ TEASPOON BLACK PEPPER
1 TABLESPOON OLIVE OIL
1 MEDIUM ONION, FINELY CHOPPED
1 SMALL CARROT, THINLY SLICED
1 SMALL CELERY RIB, THINLY SLICED
1 LARGE GREEN BELL PEPPER, CUT INTO
    ½-INCH SQUARES
1 SMALL RED BELL PEPPER, CUT INTO
    ½-INCH SQUARES

5 GARLIC CLOVES, MINCED
2 TEASPOONS MINCED FRESH OREGANO,
    OR ¾ TEASPOON DRIED
1 TEASPOON FRESH THYME, OR
    ¼ TEASPOON DRIED
ONE 28-OUNCE CAN NO-SALT-ADDED
    WHOLE TOMATOES, COARSELY
    CHOPPED, JUICE RESERVED
½ CUP DRY WHITE WINE
2 TABLESPOONS CHOPPED PARSLEY

1. Rub the chicken with ⅛ teaspoon each of the salt and black pepper. In an ovenproof skillet, warm the oil over medium-high heat. Add the chicken and brown on all sides, about 12 minutes. Transfer to a plate and set aside.

2. Reduce the heat to medium. Add the onion, carrot, celery, bell peppers, and garlic to the skillet. Sprinkle the oregano and thyme over the vegetables, and sauté until the peppers are softened, about 5 minutes. Preheat the oven to 325°.

3. Add the tomatoes (but not the juice) to the skillet, increase the heat to medium-high, and stir until the excess liquid evaporates, about 7 minutes.

4. Add the wine and the reserved tomato juice. Simmer until the liquid is reduced by one-third, about 10 minutes. Return the drumsticks to the pan, immersing them in the sauce. Season with the remaining ⅛ teaspoon each salt and black pepper.

5. Cover the skillet and bake the drumsticks for 30 minutes, or until the meat is tender and clings loosely to the bone. Transfer the drumsticks to a deep platter.

6. Place the skillet on the stovetop over high heat. Add the parsley and cook, uncovered, until the liquid is reduced by one-third, about 5 minutes. Spoon the sauce over the drumsticks and serve hot.

JAMBALAYA

SERVES 4

2 TABLESPOONS UNSALTED BUTTER

4 HOT ITALIAN SAUSAGES, CUT INTO ½-INCH PIECES (ABOUT 10 OUNCES TOTAL)

1 CUP DICED BAKED OR BOILED HAM

1 LARGE GREEN BELL PEPPER, COARSELY CHOPPED

1 LARGE CELERY RIB, COARSELY CHOPPED

2 LARGE ONIONS, COARSELY CHOPPED

2 GARLIC CLOVES, MINCED

¼ CUP MINCED PARSLEY

2 CUPS NO-SALT-ADDED CANNED WHOLE TOMATOES, WITH JUICE

¼ TEASPOON THYME

¼ TEASPOON CAYENNE PEPPER

¼ TEASPOON BLACK PEPPER

PINCH OF GROUND CLOVES

½ POUND MEDIUM SHRIMP, SHELLED AND DEVEINED

2 CUPS CHICKEN BROTH, PREFERABLY REDUCED-SODIUM

1 CUP RICE

1. In a large skillet, warm the butter over medium heat until melted. Add the sausages and ham, and sauté until the sausages are browned, 5 to 7 minutes.

2. Add the bell pepper, celery, onions, garlic, and 2 tablespoons of the parsley, and cook, stirring frequently, until the onions are softened and translucent, about 5 minutes.

3. Stir in the tomatoes, breaking them up with the back of a spoon. Add the thyme, cayenne, black pepper, cloves, shrimp, and broth, and bring to a boil.

4. Add the rice, reduce the heat to low, cover, and simmer, stirring occasionally, until the rice is tender, 25 to 30 minutes.

5. Divide the jambalaya among 4 plates and garnish with the remaining 2 tablespoons parsley.

Substitution: *In Louisiana, home of jambalaya, the sausage of choice for this dish would be andouille, a robustly spiced and smoked pork sausage. If you can get andouille, by all means use it.*

Super Chunky Hash

SERVES 4

♦ EXTRA-QUICK

1 POUND UNPEELED RED POTATOES,
CUT INTO 1-INCH CUBES

2 MEDIUM CARROTS, CUT INTO
½-INCH DICE

2 TABLESPOONS OLIVE OIL

2 TABLESPOONS UNSALTED BUTTER

8 SCALLIONS, COARSELY CHOPPED

3 GARLIC CLOVES, MINCED

1 POUND ROAST BEEF, CUT INTO
¾-INCH CUBES

2 CELERY RIBS, COARSELY CHOPPED

¼ CUP KETCHUP

2 TABLESPOONS WORCESTERSHIRE
SAUCE

1½ TEASPOONS THYME

¼ TEASPOON BLACK PEPPER

PINCH OF CAYENNE PEPPER

¼ CUP CHOPPED PARSLEY (OPTIONAL)

1. Steam the potatoes and carrots in a vegetable steamer until the vegetables are tender, about 15 minutes.

2. Meanwhile, in a large skillet, warm 1 tablespoon of the oil and 1 tablespoon of the butter over medium-high heat until the butter is melted. Add the scallions and garlic, and cook, stirring frequently, until the mixture is fragrant, 2 to 3 minutes. Transfer the scallion mixture to a plate and set aside.

3. Add the remaining 1 tablespoon each oil and butter to the pan. Add the potatoes, carrots, roast beef, and celery, and cook, stirring frequently, until the potatoes are golden, about 7 minutes.

4. Stir in the ketchup, Worcestershire sauce, thyme, black pepper, and cayenne, and cook until the flavors are blended, 1 to 2 minutes. Return the scallion mixture to the pan and stir to blend. Stir in the parsley (if using) just before serving.

Biscuit-Topped Beef Stew

SERVES 6

2 CUPS BEEF BROTH

2 TABLESPOONS TOMATO PASTE

2 TABLESPOONS DIJON MUSTARD

2 GARLIC CLOVES, MINCED

1 TEASPOON BASIL

½ TEASPOON BLACK PEPPER

1 POUND SMALL UNPEELED RED
POTATOES, THICKLY SLICED

1½ POUNDS STEW BEEF, CUT INTO
BITE-SIZE PIECES

2 MEDIUM CARROTS, CUT INTO 1-INCH
PIECES

1 MEDIUM ONION, CUT INTO THIN
WEDGES

2 CUPS FLOUR

¼ CUP GRATED PARMESAN CHEESE

2 TEASPOONS BAKING POWDER

½ TEASPOON SALT

4 TABLESPOONS COLD UNSALTED
BUTTER, CUT INTO PIECES

⅔ CUP LOW-FAT MILK

¼ CUP CHOPPED PARSLEY (OPTIONAL)

1 TABLESPOON CORNSTARCH

2 CUPS FROZEN CORN KERNELS

1. In a large ovenproof skillet or Dutch oven, bring the broth, 1 cup of water, the tomato paste, mustard, garlic, basil, and ¼ teaspoon of the pepper to a boil over medium-high heat. Add the potatoes and beef, cover, return to a boil, reduce the heat to medium-low, and simmer for 10 minutes.

2. Add the carrots and onion. Cover, increase the heat to medium-high, and return to a boil. Reduce the heat to medium-low and simmer while you make the biscuit dough.

3. Preheat the oven to 425°. In a food processor, combine the flour, Parmesan, baking powder, salt, and remaining ¼ teaspoon pepper. Pulse briefly to combine. Blend in the butter until the mixture resembles coarse

meal. Pour in the milk and process just until the dough balls up. Add the parsley (if using) and pulse just to combine.

4. In a small bowl, combine the cornstarch with 2 tablespoons of water and stir to blend. Increase the heat under the stew to medium-high and return it to a boil. Stir in the corn. Stir in the cornstarch mixture and cook, stirring constantly, until the stew thickens slightly, about 3 minutes.

5. Using about ½ cup of dough for each, form the dough into 6 biscuits and place them on top of the stew. Place the skillet in the oven and bake for 14 minutes, or until the biscuits are golden.

Oven-Braised Country Captain

SERVES 4

1 TABLESPOON OLIVE OIL

2½ TO 3 POUNDS CHICKEN PARTS

2 TABLESPOONS UNSALTED BUTTER

1 LARGE ONION, THINLY SLICED

1 LARGE GREEN BELL PEPPER, CUT INTO
THIN STRIPS

2 GARLIC CLOVES, MINCED

2 TEASPOONS CURRY POWDER, OR
MORE TO TASTE

ONE 16-OUNCE CAN NO-SALT-ADDED
WHOLE TOMATOES

1 TEASPOON BLACK PEPPER

¾ TEASPOON SALT

½ TEASPOON THYME

2 TABLESPOONS RAISINS

¼ CUP SLICED ALMONDS, TOASTED

2 TABLESPOONS MINCED PARSLEY

MANGO CHUTNEY (OPTIONAL)

1. Preheat the oven to 350°.

2. In a large ovenproof skillet, warm the oil over medium heat. Add the chicken and brown on all sides, about 10 minutes. Transfer the chicken to a plate and set aside.

3. Add the butter to the skillet and warm over medium heat until melted. Add the onion, bell pepper, garlic, and curry powder, and sauté, stirring, until the onion is softened, about 3 minutes. Add the tomatoes, black pepper, salt, and thyme, and break up the tomatoes with the back of a spoon. Simmer, uncovered, for 10 minutes.

4. Return the chicken (and any juices that have collected on the plate) to the skillet and baste it well with the sauce. Remove the skillet from the heat, cover, place in the oven, and bake for 20 minutes.

5. Add the raisins to the skillet and stir to combine. Cover and bake for 10 minutes, or until the chicken is cooked through.

6. When ready to serve, sprinkle the chicken with the toasted almonds and minced parsley. Serve with chutney on the side, if desired.

KITCHEN NOTE: *Country Captain is believed to have originated with a Southern sea captain who brought back the flavors of India to his home port. For a proper Indian meal, you'll want to serve the chicken with (or over) steaming-hot rice.*

BACON, LETTUCE, AND TOMATO STRATA

SERVES 6

1 TABLESPOON VEGETABLE OIL

1 MEDIUM ONION, COARSELY CHOPPED

10 SLICES OF WHOLE WHEAT OR WHITE BREAD

2 MEDIUM TOMATOES, CUT INTO ¼-INCH-THICK SLICES

2 CUPS SHREDDED CHEDDAR CHEESE (ABOUT ½ POUND)

5 EGGS

2 CUPS LOW-FAT MILK

1 TABLESPOON DIJON MUSTARD

½ TEASPOON SALT

¼ TEASPOON BLACK PEPPER

4 SLICES OF BACON

2 LETTUCE LEAVES, SHREDDED

1. In a medium skillet, warm the oil over medium heat. Add the onion and sauté until softened, 1 to 2 minutes. Remove from the heat.

2. Butter a shallow 13 x 9-inch baking dish. Arrange half of the bread in the prepared dish. Top with half the tomatoes and half the cheese. Repeat the layering, ending with the cheese.

3. In a large bowl, lightly beat the eggs. Add the sautéed onion, the milk, mustard, salt, and pepper. Pour the egg mixture over the ingredients in the baking dish. Cover and refrigerate for 1 hour or overnight.

4. Preheat the oven to 350°. Bake the strata, uncovered, for 50 minutes, or until puffed and golden and a knife inserted in the center comes out clean. Let stand for 10 minutes before cutting.

5. Meanwhile, in a medium skillet, cook the bacon over medium heat until crisp, about 10 minutes. Drain the bacon on paper towels, then crumble.

6. Serve the strata garnished with the shredded lettuce and crumbled bacon.

Tex-Mex Macaroni and Cheese

SERVES 4

2 CUPS SMALL ELBOW MACARONI

2 TABLESPOONS UNSALTED BUTTER

3 TABLESPOONS FLOUR

1 TEASPOON DRY MUSTARD

¼ TEASPOON SALT

2 CUPS LOW-FAT MILK

2 CUPS SHREDDED LONGHORN OR
   OTHER MILD CHEDDAR CHEESE

¼ CUP CANNED DICED MILD GREEN
   CHILIES

1 TEASPOON WORCESTERSHIRE SAUCE

1 TABLESPOON OLIVE OIL

½ CUP CHOPPED SCALLIONS

1 TEASPOON CHILI POWDER

ONE 8-OUNCE CAN TOMATO SAUCE

¼ CUP PITTED SLICED BLACK OLIVES
   (OPTIONAL)

1. Preheat the oven to 375°. Butter a shallow 1½-quart baking dish.

2. In a large pot of boiling water, cook the macaroni until al dente according to package directions.

3. Meanwhile, in a medium saucepan, warm the butter over medium heat until melted. Whisk in the flour, mustard, and salt. Remove the pan from the heat and gradually whisk in the milk. Return the pan to medium heat and cook, whisking constantly, until the sauce is thickened, about 3 minutes. Reduce the heat to low and simmer the sauce for 1 minute.

4. Remove from the heat and stir in 1½ cups of the cheese, the chilies, and Worcestershire sauce. Cook, stirring constantly, until the cheese melts, about 2 minutes; set aside.

5. Drain the macaroni and return it to the cooking pot, add the cheese sauce, and toss well. Transfer the mixture to the prepared baking dish, smooth the top, and bake for 25 to 30 minutes, or until the sauce is bubbling.

6. Meanwhile, in a small saucepan, warm the oil over medium heat. Add ¼ cup of the scallions and the chili powder, and sauté for 1 minute. Stir in the tomato sauce and bring to a boil. Reduce the heat to low, partially cover, and simmer for 10 minutes.

7. Remove the baked macaroni from the oven, spoon the tomato sauce down the center, and top with the remaining ½ cup cheese and ¼ cup scallions. Sprinkle with the olives (if using) and serve hot.

Southwestern Lasagna

SERVES 8

2 TABLESPOONS OLIVE OIL

2 MEDIUM ONIONS, COARSELY
CHOPPED

2 GARLIC CLOVES, MINCED

ONE 28-OUNCE CAN NO-SALT-ADDED
WHOLE TOMATOES

ONE 8-OUNCE CAN TOMATO SAUCE

ONE 4-OUNCE CAN CHOPPED MILD
GREEN CHILIES (OPTIONAL)

3 TABLESPOONS CHILI POWDER

1 TABLESPOON CUMIN

½ TEASPOON SALT

½ TEASPOON BLACK PEPPER

1 POUND LASAGNA NOODLES

½ POUND MONTEREY JACK CHEESE,
SHREDDED

¾ CUP GRATED PARMESAN CHEESE

1 POUND LOW-FAT COTTAGE CHEESE,
PREFERABLY SMALL CURD

1. In a medium saucepan, combine the oil, onions, and garlic, and cook over medium-high heat for 5 minutes.

2. Add the tomatoes, tomato sauce, chilies (if using), chili powder, cumin, salt, and pepper, and break up the tomatoes with the back of a spoon. Bring the mixture to a simmer, reduce the heat to medium-low, and simmer, stirring occasionally, until the sauce is thickened, about 35 minutes.

3. Meanwhile, in a large pot of boiling water, cook the lasagna noodles until al dente according to package directions. Rinse the noodles under cold water and drain well.

4. Preheat the oven to 350°. In a medium bowl, toss the Monterey jack and Parmesan together.

5. Spoon some sauce into a 13 x 9-inch baking dish. Make three layers, using the following sequence of ingredients: noodles, cottage cheese, sauce, and shredded cheese mixture (using only about three-fourths of the cheese mixture).

6. Top the lasagna with any remaining sauce and the remaining cheese mixture. Bake for 35 minutes, or until the filling is bubbling. Let stand for 15 minutes before serving.

Baked Ziti

SERVES 4 TO 6

2 TABLESPOONS OLIVE OIL

½ CUP CHOPPED ONION

ONE 28-OUNCE CAN NO-SALT-ADDED
WHOLE TOMATOES IN PURÉE

¼ CUP TOMATO PASTE

1 BAY LEAF

½ TEASPOON OREGANO

½ TEASPOON BASIL

PINCH OF SUGAR

¾ TEASPOON SALT

¼ TEASPOON BLACK PEPPER

¾ POUND LEAN GROUND BEEF

¾ CUP CHOPPED PARSLEY

½ CUP FINE UNSEASONED DRY BREAD
CRUMBS

¼ CUP GRATED PARMESAN CHEESE

1 EGG

¾ POUND ZITI

½ POUND SHREDDED PART-SKIM
MOZZARELLA CHEESE

1 CUP PART-SKIM RICOTTA CHEESE

1. In a medium saucepan, warm the oil over medium heat. Add the onion and sauté, stirring occasionally, until softened, about 2 minutes. Stir in the tomatoes and break them up with the back of a spoon. Stir in the tomato paste, bay leaf, oregano, basil, sugar, ¼ teaspoon of the salt, and ⅛ teaspoon of the pepper, and bring to a simmer.

2. Crumble the beef into a large bowl. Add ½ cup of the parsley, the bread crumbs, Parmesan, and the remaining ½ teaspoon salt and ⅛ teaspoon pepper. Stir in the egg. With wet hands, shape the mixture into 1-inch meatballs. You will have about 30 meatballs.

3. Drop the meatballs into the sauce and simmer gently, uncovered, turning them occasionally, for 20 minutes.

4. Meanwhile, in a large pot of boiling water, cook the ziti until al dente according to package directions. Drain well.

5. Preheat the oven to 375°.

6. Remove and discard the bay leaf from the sauce. Transfer half of the tomato sauce and meatballs to a 13 x 9-inch baking pan. Spread the ziti over the sauce. Top the ziti with the mozzarella and the remaining sauce and meatballs. Dot with spoonfuls of the ricotta cheese and bake for 20 minutes, or until piping hot.

7. Serve the baked ziti sprinkled with the remaining ¼ cup parsley.

Broccoli and Smoked Turkey Gratin

SERVES 6

3 TABLESPOONS UNSALTED BUTTER

¼ CUP FLOUR

1 CUP LOW-FAT MILK

½ TEASPOON NUTMEG

¼ TEASPOON BLACK PEPPER

2 CUPS SHREDDED SWISS CHEESE

¼ CUP GRATED ROMANO OR PARMESAN CHEESE

2 TABLESPOONS DIJON MUSTARD

ONE 10-OUNCE PACKAGE FROZEN CHOPPED BROCCOLI, THAWED AND SQUEEZED DRY

¾ POUND SMOKED TURKEY, CUT INTO ¾-INCH CUBES

8 SCALLIONS, COARSELY CHOPPED

1 TABLESPOON FINE UNSEASONED DRY BREAD CRUMBS

1. Preheat the oven to 375°. Lightly oil a shallow 11 x 7-inch baking dish.

2. In a medium saucepan, warm the butter over medium heat until melted. Stir in the flour and cook, stirring constantly, until the flour is no longer visible, about 30 seconds. Stir in the milk, nutmeg, and pepper, and cook, stirring, until the mixture is thickened, about 3 minutes.

3. Stir in 1½ cups of the Swiss cheese, the Romano, and mustard. Remove from the heat.

4. Stir the broccoli, turkey, and scallions into the saucepan. Pour this mixture into the prepared baking dish. Sprinkle the top with the bread crumbs and the remaining ½ cup Swiss cheese.

5. Bake the gratin for 30 minutes, or until the filling is hot and the top is light golden.

Variation: *Rather than using smoked turkey, make this casserole with plain roast turkey, but keep the smoky flavor by substituting a smoked cheese (such as Gouda) for the Swiss cheese. Choose Romano rather than Parmesan, as it has a more robust flavor.*

CAROLINA SHRIMP PIE

SERVES 4

1 EGG

¾ CUP LOW-FAT MILK

5 SLICES FIRM-TEXTURED WHITE
    BREAD, CUT INTO CUBES

3 TABLESPOONS UNSALTED BUTTER

4 SCALLIONS, COARSELY CHOPPED

1 LARGE GREEN BELL PEPPER, DICED

2 GARLIC CLOVES, MINCED

1 POUND SHRIMP—SHELLED,
    DEVEINED, AND COARSELY CHOPPED

1 TABLESPOON SHERRY (OPTIONAL)

2 TEASPOONS WORCESTERSHIRE SAUCE

3 DROPS OF HOT PEPPER SAUCE

½ TEASPOON SALT

¼ TEASPOON BLACK PEPPER

3 TABLESPOONS FINE UNSEASONED
    DRY BREAD CRUMBS

1. Preheat the oven to 375°. Butter a 1-quart baking dish.

2. In a medium bowl, beat the egg and milk together. Add the bread cubes and toss to coat well. Set aside.

3. In a medium skillet, warm 2 tablespoons of the butter over medium-high heat until melted. Add the scallions, bell pepper, and garlic, and cook until the vegetables are softened and the garlic is beginning to brown, about 7 minutes.

4. Scrape the scallion-pepper mixture into the bowl with the bread cube mixture. Add the shrimp, sherry (if using), Worcestershire sauce, hot pepper sauce, salt, and black pepper, and toss to combine.

5. Transfer the mixture to the prepared baking dish and sprinkle the bread crumbs on top. Melt the butter and drizzle over the bread crumbs.

6. Bake for 25 minutes, or until the top of the pie is golden.

✦ Index